PRECIOUS WILLIAMS

PRECIOUS

- A True Story -

BLOOMSBURY
LONDON · BERLIN · NEW YORK

First published in Great Britain 2010

Bloomsbury Publishing Plc
36 Soho Square
London W1D 3QY

www.bloomsbury.com

Bloomsbury Publishing, London, New York and Berlin

A CIP catalogue record for this book is available from the British Library

ISBN 978 0 7475 8421 6

10 9 8 7 6 5 4 3 2 1

Typeset by Hewer Text UK Ltd, Edinburgh
Printed in Great Britain by Clays Limited, St Ives plc

Mixed Sources
Product group from well-managed
forests and other controlled sources
www.fsc.org Cert no. SGS-COC-2061
© 1996 Forest Stewardship Council
FSC

PRECIOUS

With love to my daughter – I hope you will come to realise
how precious you are.

Book One

It cannot be expected that this system of farming would produce any very extraordinary or luxuriant crop.

Charles Dickens, *Oliver Twist*

1971

THIS, I AM TOLD, is how it begins.

It's September.

A tall black woman with a foreign accent pulls up to the kerb in a red convertible. She parks on a tree-lined street, on a council estate in rural West Sussex. The stocky, espresso-skinned man next to her keeps twisting round in his seat to gaze at the plump baby girl asleep in a Moses basket on the back seat.

The woman's gold bracelets jangle as she switches off the ignition, rolls on an extra layer of lip gloss and adjusts the mirror to pout at her reflection. Unknown to her, net curtains begin to rustle and twitch. White faces peer out. Wondering. Watching.

The woman slams her car door shut. She strides down the little dandelion-choked path to number 52, West Walk, her flat nose tipped towards the setting sun. The man trails several steps behind her. The woman, in her white silk suit, turns and adjusts the lapel of her companion's sports jacket.

The front door opens.

The black woman, almost six feet tall, towers over the white woman standing in front of her.

'Mrs Taylor?' the tall stranger enquires.

Mrs Taylor says she prefers to be called Nanny. 'The children like it.'

Nanny is nearly fifty-seven years old, silver-haired, eyes the colour of clouds on a rainy day. Five feet tall.

*   *   *

3

Nanny had sent away for the baby in the Moses basket a few days earlier. She had been sending away for African children and looking after them in her home for more than a decade. But when the last two, brothers named Babatunde and Onyeka, were abruptly taken back by their natural parents, Nanny promised herself she'd stop. Children coming and going simply caused her too much heartbreak.

Despite that, she still browsed wistfully through the classified ads in the back pages of *Nursery World* magazine, just to see the latest African children on offer. That's where she found the infant now on her doorstep. The ad said, 'attractive baby girl of Nigerian origin'. Nanny couldn't resist.

'So you must be Mrs . . .' says Nanny, her thin, pale skin blooming with excitement. She does not know how to pronounce the woman's name. 'I'm glad you found us all right. Come in, come in.'

The woman smiles and stoops slightly in her heels to enter. The man follows her in, clutching the Moses basket.

'Please. Call me Lizzy,' she says. 'And this is her. Her name's Anita-Precious,' she continues, looking absently down at the baby, as if she has just remembered it existed.

'Let me have a dekko at her then,' says Nanny.

The ten-week-old baby has skin the colour of toffee and a wig-like puff of black tightly curled hair. She lies there curling and uncurling her tiny fists, her round mouth open but unsmiling.

'Oh yes, yes. She's lovely, isn't she, Lizzy?' Nanny coos.

Lizzy remains silent. She has a put-out, nauseated look on her face. Like someone who's just trodden in dog's mess while wearing their favourite shoes.

So here I am: the silent, watchful baby in a Moses basket.

Nanny falls in love with me instantly, or at least that's what she tells me once I'm old enough to ask about my past.

Gramps, Nanny's lovely husband, sits in his wheelchair, smiling rather than talking. His lips no longer work as well as they once did. So when he does speak, his words slide out in a slur. He manages to ask this flawlessly turned-out couple where they come from in Africa. The woman answers for the pair of them. *Nigeria.* Gramps nods approvingly. Like he's been there.

The sitting room is blue and it coordinates with Nanny, in her blue nylon shirtwaister dress, with the iridescent butterfly brooch on her lapel. Nanny's daughter, Wendy, is perched on the end of the blue sofa. Wendy. So slim she's nicknamed Olive Oyl. Long, straight, near-black hair. Skin tanned from the long summer. Eager to hold the brand-new black baby.

Wendy's wearing an outfit - purple suede fringed coat and flared jeans - that Nanny's written off as 'absolutely ridiculous'. But despite her hippie gear, Wendy's not trying to be a hippie. The most important thing in the world to her is simply becoming a mother. One day.

Wendy's fiancé, Mick, whose hair's even longer than hers - he is here too. His hazel eyes sweep from the baby to the stiff-looking black bloke to the scarily glamorous black lady - inches taller than he is - who is staring right back at him.

The black couple stays for about an hour that day. The man, whose name turns out to be Rupert, sits there making jittery small-talk. Asking Mick about his job as a caretaker at the local secondary school. Nobody asks who Rupert is - whether he's the baby's father; whether he's the mother's husband. They presume he is somehow significant since he's there.

My mother carries out an inspection of the three-bedroom council house, briskly appraising the room that will become mine. That done, she curls her sinewy frame into a blue armchair and poses there, calm and elegantly disinterested; not asking anyone many questions, other than how much this placement is going to cost her.

There is a drawn-out conversation about money that day, all in hushed tones, as if the grown-ups are afraid a three-month-old baby could understand their words.

I picture them haggling.

Lizzy quotes the sum she is prepared to pay.

'I can't do it for that, Lizzy,' Nanny says.

'Seven fifty a week then,' says Lizzy, offering the lower end of the going-rate for private foster care at that time. 'It is the most I can afford.'

Nanny is calling Lizzy's bluff – she'd have taken me off Lizzy's hands for free if necessary.

Later, years later, I will ask Nanny and Wendy and Mick what my mother was like that very first time they met her. What they made of her. Wendy will recall, 'She was always such a lovely looking woman your mother. Ever so intelligent. So beautifully dressed.'

Mick will say, 'She seemed nice enough, didn't she? *Then.*'

Nanny will say, '*Very* high-faluting. Right from the start. Walked into my house like she bloody well owned it.'

My mother will eventually claim, 'Something about that place, that whole environment, it made my skin crawl.'

But this feeling she has doesn't prevent my mother, a reluctant-looking Rupert by her side, returning to Fernmere two or three days later with me in a Moses basket on the back seat of the convertible. And this time, when the pair drives back to their own house in London, the back seat is empty.

1976

I SIT IN NANNY'S lap, trying to conjure up an image of my mother. In our house, we've no photos of Mummy Elizabeth, as I call her. When I think about her, which is every day, the main memories of her that spring to my mind are the juicy-fruit smell of her breath, the humungous gap between her teeth – and her witch-like laughter.

Mummy Elizabeth vanished several months ago. At the time, Nanny said maybe she'd buggered off back to Africa and abandoned me once and for all. But, no, it turns out Mummy Elizabeth's now returned to her house in London and she has rung and instructed us to sit tight until she arrives to take us out for a slap-up lunch (or dinner, depending on what time she arrives).

Peeking through the sitting-room window, I await Mummy Elizabeth's arrival. I feel the same as when I'm watching my favourite film, *The Wizard of Oz*, when I hold my breath through the scenes right before the Wicked Witch of the West appears. Terror, like ice in the pit of my stomach, makes me want to close my eyes or run and hide and scream, but also, perversely, makes me long for the moment when the witch appears.

I look over at Gramps. He is sitting in his wheelchair with his eyelids drooping. I wonder what he thinks of my mother suddenly coming back into our lives.

'What time's she getting here, Nanny?'

'Knowing her she'll take her own sweet time.'

'What does my mother *do* when she's in Africa, Nanny?'

'How on earth should *I* know, love?'

I picture Mummy Elizabeth in Africa, wearing a loincloth. I see her dancing round a six-foot-high fire, flanked by roaring chee-tahs. She kicks her heron-like legs in time to the drumbeats, then splays her knees as she limbo dances to the ground and slides onto her back at the fire's edge, cackling so hard the cheetahs grow afraid of her.

'You're shivering, love,' says Nanny. 'Why don't you go and fetch your white cardigan and slip it on?'

'I'm not cold, thanks,' I say.

I'm hot. It is so sunny that everything's tinged yellow. One of those days like a sherbert dip, fizzing and bubbling on for ever, never seeming to quite dissolve, till in the time it takes to blink, it turns dark and the kids now playing outside on their skates will disappear inside houses just like ours for their tea.

My pink party dress is beginning to cling to my heavily greased skin. Nanny has really gone to town with my appearance, coating my hair, face and body with Johnson's Baby Oil, primping me for Mummy Elizabeth with the same vigour she uses to prepare a chicken for the oven.

'Do you think my mother will like me this time, Nanny?'

'Well, she should do; you're absolutely gorgeous, darling.'

Last time Mummy Elizabeth came, which was before I'd started primary school, she was very unhappy with the way I was turning out. I couldn't carry on a conversation at all, she said, and my hair looked like a hedge, my skin was ashy, my eyes were dull and my personality even duller. Most of all, she didn't like the fact that I screamed 'No!' whenever one of the uncles she brought to visit tried to speak to me, or hug me.

One of the uncles I'm most scared of is this one called Uncle Chucky, who she often brings. Behind his back, Nanny calls him 'that vicious coloured gentleman'. Uncle Chucky wears shoes made of white lizard skin and he picks at his teeth with a series of cocktail sticks I feel sure he's snatched from sausages at birthday parties. His other speciality is whipping a metal-pronged Afro comb out of his pocket when you're least expecting it and then pointing it at you like a weapon.

They fill our house with noise when they arrive, the Africans. Foreign voices soaring, mean laughter whistling through the gap in Mummy Elizabeth's teeth. If Uncle Chucky's among them, he'll grin at me, revealing teeth as white as his shoes. Then he'll keep going: 'Anita-oh!' for absolutely no reason. And he'll say, 'Come. Let me fix your hair,' and reach into his back pocket to take out the Afro comb.

I always yell, 'Nooo!' and then I sit there trying not to cry.

It's the same whenever they come. My mother's surrounded by other Africans and there's always one of them who'll pull out a comb and offer to do my hair. My very earliest memory is of one of the Africans' visits. I am about to turn three. I remember my mother sweeping in, dressed in pale silk, smelling like the perfume counter at Boots. One of my uncles at her side, reaching out to try to hug me.

'Go on,' Mummy Elizabeth instructs. 'Go to him.'

'I can't,' I say.

'What do you mean, you *can't*? Let him do your hair. Your hair is a disgrace. It must be combed!' says Mummy Elizabeth.

I look at the comb's silvery prongs. I look up at Nanny and Nanny looks down at the carpet.

'*Behave*, Anita,' Mummy Elizabeth screams.

'I can't,' I say.

'Can't?' Mummy Elizabeth's voice rises, octaves above its usual contralto. '*Can't?*'

Nanny looks up, her eyes like chips of colourless crystal.

'She's a shy little thing, Lizzy,' Nanny says. 'She's not used to being around a lot of men, apart from my useless son-in-law, Mick.' Nanny lets out a hoarse, choked little laugh.

Mummy Elizabeth stalks across our sitting room so purposefully that our coffee table rattles. She takes my hand. Her hand's so silky and smooth it seems wet as it slides up my wrist. She grabs on to my elbow, and my arm stretches out of its socket as Mummy Elizabeth leads me outside, along the garden path. The weeds tickle my legs.

'You are just *horrible*, Anita,' Mummy Elizabeth screams. 'And I am sick of it. *Sick of it!*'

Mummy Elizabeth drags me by the arm, down the garden path. My feet dangling; summer sandal falling off into the unchecked weeds below. My mother is wearing her high-heeled Italian shoes. She has pairs and pairs, in a variety of colours. Her pride and joy. She kicks at me. Her high heel sinks into the soft spot where my bottom connects with my thigh. She kicks me again. Again, spiky heel meets plump, toddler flesh.

'For the love of God, Lizzy! Stop it! Stop it,' pleads Nanny. 'I can't *bear* it. *Stop it!*'

Mummy Elizabeth keeps kicking.

And Aunty Wendy falls to her knees. She is expecting a baby. Aunty Wendy begins feeling wave-like pains, like period pains times one hundred thousand. Seven months gone. The pains aren't allowed to come yet.

My mother kicks me again. My mother's not happy; but then, it seems, she rarely is. It is my fault entirely. I asked for this. I failed to walk to Mummy Elizabeth's car fast enough. I was dawdling and crying and flinching and Mummy Elizabeth had no choice but to discipline me.

Aunty Wendy's pains won't stop. Neither will my mother. Someone must call a doctor. An ambulance. The police?

Something has to be done. Aunty Wendy must be rushed to hospital. My mother should be stopped. Why isn't my mother being stopped?

Nanny later recalls this day. She says Mummy Elizabeth continued to kick me down the garden path. All *I* remember, after the first few kicks, was feeling weightless, feeling a fragment of my normal size, and finally becoming a little worm, burrowing beneath the dandelions, into the soil and out of sight.

The man they call Rupert snatched me from Mummy Elizabeth's arms and dashed up the path, a hero out of a Western movie, minus the Stetson. He placed me in Nanny's flaccid arms. Nanny closed the door. Phone calls were made. I was bruised but the skin wasn't broken. Wagon Wheels were fed to me. No one asked if *I* was broken. Aunty Wendy was taken to hospital; Uncle Mick was informed. Gramps said nothing at all, but he cried. And cried.

'I feel scared, Nanny,' I say.

'There's no need to. You know I won't let anything bad happen to you, darling.'

I know nothing of the kind. When Nanny and I say our prayers together at night, right before we say Amen, she asks Gentle Jesus to help make sure I'm always safe from harm. I believe Jesus wants to protect me, but I already know that Nanny won't, or can't. When my mother kicked me, Nanny and Aunty Wendy stood there unmoving, crying for my mother to stop. In my eyes, they were watching and not doing anything.

I sink into Nanny's lap. The glare of the sun has tinted my bare legs a golden honey colour. Nanny's skin is as dry, flaky and pale as uncooked pastry and next to hers, my skin looks dark like a shadow.

She's always telling me, 'Your colour doesn't matter, Anita. You're just the same as me underneath.'

But I'm not the same as Nanny. I wish she was my real Nanny, but she's not. I know this because I have heard grown-ups whisper among themselves, 'Oh, she must be Mrs Taylor's latest little foster child.'

'She's not coming, love,' Nanny says.

'What do you mean, Nanny?'

'Your mother. It's gone nine o'clock, love. It's past your bedtime.'

'She *is* coming, Nanny,' I say. 'I *know* she is.'

'How do you know, darling?'

'She was in my dream just now when I had my nap. She kept kissing me and she said how much I've grown and how good I am at talking and not being shy now. She had hair right down to her waist, Nanny. Like Rapunzel.'

'Oh, you do have an imagination on you,' says Nanny. 'How could a coloured woman possibly have hair down to her waist? Chance would be a fine thing.'

'She did. She *is* coming, Nanny.'

The truth is, I need Mummy Elizabeth to come. She petrifies me, but my need to believe that my mother loves me and wants me is even greater than my fear of her. It's vital to me to be able to tell my friends at school, with pretend casualness, 'My mum's coming down to take me out at the weekend.' Then, when one of the bullies on our estate corners me and sneers, 'Even your own mum don't want you, you little nig-nog reject,' I can hold my head up and think, *You're wrong. You're wrong about me.*

'I'm sorry, darling, but she's not coming,' Nanny says and her voice has a finality to it that keeps my mouth shut. 'We'll have to let Wendy know, love. Go and get your shoes on, darling.'

Aunty Wendy doesn't have a phone. The only way to relay news to her is to nip round to her house, a two-minute trot away. It's dark and the trees look like black skeletons. But it's still so hot that the tarmac warms my heels where they poke over the scrunched backs of my plimsolls. As I run someone says 'Oi, oi' and I see a big boy called Wayne standing in front of me, blocking my path.

He pokes out his elbows, pretends to be scratching inside his armpits, his huge mouth forms into an O and he goes, 'Ooo-oo-oo! Look at this fuckin' little chimp runnin'! Where you off to in such a hurry then, you little nig-nog?'

'Nowhere,' I reply.

'What?'

'Nothing.'

I run and don't stop running until I reach Aunty Wendy's front door, which opens before I can even ring the doorbell.

'Aunty Wendy!'

'All right, love? Don't *you* look smart! What you all worked up about then? Your mother been already, has she?'

'She hasn't turned up again. My mother! She's not coming!'

'What? *Again?*' says Aunty Wendy. 'It's a bloody disgrace. Ought to be ashamed of herself! You coming in then, love?'

The Kid Factory

FOR A WHILE, I am the only coloured girl in the town, but I'm not the only coloured child the town has ever seen.

Since the 1960s there's been a little stream of African babies and toddlers being dropped off at the homes of white strangers in West Sussex. Both Nanny and Aunty Wendy have had many private foster babies – almost all of them African and most of them Nigerian.

Those of us not advertised in *Nursery World* are advertised on postcards in shop windows. Anyone can send off for us and we begin popping up in white homes throughout the country, especially in Hampshire, Kent, Surrey, Middlesex, Essex and Sussex.

Few questions are asked of birth parent or foster-parent. Social Services are supposed to be notified, but often aren't. When alerted, social workers do have to call round periodically to check the coloured foster-kids are being fed, clothed and sent to school – but the foster-parents don't have to be registered, trained or checked by the police.

Later, in the 1980s, our numbers in West Sussex will mushroom as more and more local white families catch on to the trend. A boy at my secondary school will brag, 'We just got one of your lot. Got a bigger knob than a grown man, he has. Made him flop it out for my gran because she wouldn't believe us till she saw it.'

Private fostering is supposed to be strictly temporary. The birth parents are often recent immigrants from West Africa. Typically they are full-time students by day, struggling to make ends meet by working one or even two night jobs, striving to create a secure home for their children. Once their studies are completed and their financial situation begins to ease, most of them take their babies back.

My case is a little different. My mother is not, as far as we can tell, a student. She doesn't appear to be hard up and in fact she says she is from a well-heeled and titled Igbo family in Nigeria. According to her, my father is a civil engineer from a privileged Krio family in Sierra Leone. Yet at nine days old I am despatched to my first foster home, in the West Country, where my mother fails to visit me for the next two months.

By the time I reach Nanny, aged ten weeks, I am a withdrawn, watchful baby with a mysterious past. Nanny tells anyone who asks that she thinks I am a Biafran.

Throughout my infancy, I have a number of aliases. When I arrive in Fernmere, my mother introduces me as Anita-Precious Achaba. Three months later, my mother has changed my name to Precious-Anita Eze. Later I find that – according to my birth certificate – my name is actually Precious Anita Williams.

Back in the days when I'm called Anita-Precious Achaba, my mother visits once every three weeks, usually arriving with the man named Rupert, who sometimes refers to himself as my father.

When I'm eight months old, my mother appears in Fernmere with a new man and says she's taking me 'home' to Nigeria. Nanny cries and pleas with my mother to let me stay but, ignoring her, my mother sweeps upstairs to pack up my toys and clothes.

Nanny's family is used to this sort of thing happening. Her grown-up son, Dave, who's married and has his own kids, tolerates Nanny's private-fostering but certainly doesn't encourage it.

Nanny grieves for me and, several months later, begins scanning *Nursery World* magazine for a new foster child. And there I am, advertised once again in the magazine's back pages.

Shortly after my return to Nanny, West Sussex Social Services despatch a social worker with cheddar-coloured hair to see what we're all up to. In her report the social worker observes:

July 1972: Visited and was introduced to this coloured child, Precious, by Mrs Taylor. The child has so far not cried and is no trouble at all. A most attractive child.

Mrs Taylor has fostered children for a number of years. Now that she has an invalid husband to look after, she seems to derive pleasure and light relief by caring for small children, particularly Nigerian children.

A couple of years later, I am reclaimed by my mother once more. Again this reunion doesn't last long and my mother decides to return me to foster care. This time she does not advertise me in *Nursery World* but instead rings Nanny up and says, 'I'm bringing her back tomorrow. I am leaving her with you now until she is old enough for boarding school.'

Nanny greets us at the door weeping tears of joy. 'God has sent my little darling back to me,' she says.

But Nanny, having thought that my mother really had taken me for good the last time, had replaced me with a little girl from Ghana. This new girl, Effua, sleeps in my bedroom under my silky pink eiderdown. She drinks her Ribena out of my special cup with the built-in curly straw.

I watch in disbelief as this tiny stranger with the charcoal skin and close-cropped hair sits in Nanny's lap and follows Nanny around and eats Wagon Wheel after Wagon Wheel, just like I used to. She even has the nerve to constantly talk to and pester my beloved Gramps.

Effua and I won't play together nicely, the way Nanny wants us to. We either ignore one another or we scratch, pinch and scream. Nanny doesn't know what to do. At her age, she can't cope with two little girls, especially as she has an invalid husband to look after. One of us little coloured girls will have to go. I feel so threatened by Effua, so afraid Effua will become Nanny and Gramps's new little angel, that I run around the house screaming, and then I begin kicking at furniture, and at people.

Nevertheless, Nanny chooses me. I hear her telling the grown-ups she feels an 'affinity' to me. I don't know what the word means but I feel like the most important little girl in the world. Nanny begins making arrangements to get rid of Effua and I am moved back permanently into my pink bedroom.

Effua is sent to live with Aunty Wendy. A new social worker is dispatched to check up on us.

October 1974: I visited Mrs Taylor for the first time, expecting to find Precious Anita and Effua fostered by Mrs Taylor. However, Mrs Taylor and her daughter, Mrs Travis appear to have (to say the least) unorthodox views as to carrying out regulations. Effua had been moved to Mrs Taylor's daughter, Mrs Travis. We had not in fact been notified of this change. I did feel that it was rather distressing the way these coloured children were passed about from hand to hand like this.

Effua seems to thrive at Aunty Wendy's and I delight in my life at Nanny's, savouring the hugs, the gentle words, the unlimited access to Wagon Wheels. An uneasy alliance between Effua and I gradually softens into a friendship. But we continue to delight in getting one another into trouble with the grown-ups.

'Guess what, Aunty Wendy.'

We are upstairs on the double-decker back from Bognor when I begin to tug at the waistband of Aunty Wendy's maxi-skirt.

'What, love?'

'At the arcade this afternoon, when you weren't watching,' I say, 'Effua said that I was *black* and that I'll *stay* black until the day that I die.'

Effua, sitting next to me, lowers her guilty eyes to the floor.

'Aren't you going to tell Effy off for calling me black, Aunty Wendy?'

'What did you call her that for, love?' says Aunty Wendy. 'You know *black* isn't a nice word. Christ, girls, how many times do I have to tell you both? You're *not* black; you're little coloured girls.'

Bognor is not far from our town, Fernmere, but unlike Bognor we've got no beach, no cinema, no arcade and no Kentucky Fried Chicken – we've just got loads of antiques shops and building societies.

Almost everyone in Fernmere is wealthy. But we're not. Which is why we live on Woodview, the council estate, home to what the rich people call 'the riff-raff and the gypos'. Some of the posh people are actually afraid to venture 'up Woodview' because they think they might not come out alive. Yet to me Woodview is the most magical place in the whole of Fernmere.

The road to Woodview is short and narrow and bursting with greenness. On either side of the road there are blackberry and rose-hip bushes and patches of wild grass dotted with poppies and dandelion clocks. Today the bushes are shadowy and I can't see the luscious fruit hanging off them; it has grown dark early because it's pouring down. Rain slams against the pavement, sounding the way a TV does before it's been tuned to a channel; making me, Wendy and Effy run as if for our lives. Cars skid into and out of the estate, their headlights dimmed and blurred by the sheets of rain.

'Am I having tea at your house tonight, Aunty Wendy?' I ask, breathless.

'Course you are, love,'

'Yippee!'

We jog past the sign that reads Woodview Way, past the little shop that sells Cornettos and Twix bars and past West Walk, where me and Nanny live. Effua skips ahead, as always, stopping every three or four steps to splash her silly foot in a puddle, turn and giggle for no reason.

The houses we pass are all made of pale peach brick, two storeys high and joined to one another. Everything about them is perfectly square: the windows, the garages, the emerald-green portions of grass on the front lawns.

Well-to-do people, Nanny says, don't live in little boxes like these: they live in rambling, asymmetrical and sometimes crumbling big houses with names instead of numbers on the door. Nanny grew up in such a house before she lost everything and moved to Woodview. I can think of nothing more frightening than living in a large, meandering old house that might have mice in it, or worse, ghosts.

Aunty Wendy's back door opens with a squeak and then bangs shut.

Uncle Mick walks into the kitchen and over to the fridge. His corduroy flares hang down at the back and there's a bunch of keys bigger than my whole hand swinging from his belt loop.

'Hello, *Presh*,' he says, smirking.

Uncle Mick is the only person who still refers to my real name, Precious, and he only calls me it when he's making fun of me. To everyone else in Fernmere I'm Anita, Neety, Nin. To people outside our family, I'm sometimes 'that little darkie'.

'All right, Effy?' Uncle Mick says and then he quickly turns his attention back to me. 'What the bloody hell do you think you look like in that get up then?'

I'm wearing a pair of red nylon flares that are too short for me with a matching red shirt with the longest collar you've ever seen.

'Just ignore him, Neet,' says Aunty Wendy. 'You look lovely.'

I know he's only joking. Uncle Mick's always made it clear that I'm his favourite, which is a big part of why I love him so much. I'd like to call him Dad but I can't, because everyone at school knows he's not my dad and they'd make fun of me for being such a loser.

One of the things I adore most about Uncle Mick is his huge collection of dusty LPs. The faces on almost all of the covers – Diana Ross, Marvin Gaye, Smokey Robinson, the Jackson 5 – are brown like mine.

I'm deep in thought, wondering if Uncle Mick is *really* going to buy me the new Jackson 5 album for my birthday.

'What's the matter, little girl?' he says. 'Need to go home to your Nanny, do you? Afraid Nanny's worryin' about you, are ya?'

Nanny *will* be worrying about me. She'll be sitting in front of the TV wringing her hands and imagining that all sorts of bad things have happened to me. She hates not having me where she can see me. When I left her this afternoon and she stood in the doorway of our beautiful little house, watching me walk off hand-in-hand with Aunty Wendy, Nanny looked like she wanted to run up the garden path and prise me away from her daughter and take me back inside the house to sit with her all day. Not that Nanny will ever run down a garden path again. She is so full of nerves, so asthmatic and has such poorly legs that it is a great trial for her to walk. So Nanny drives almost everywhere.

When Aunty Wendy walks me back to Nanny's later, the first thing Nanny will say is: 'What did Neety eat? Did she have enough to eat?' and Aunty Wendy will recount every little thing (that she knows about) that I ate.

The second question Nanny will *always* ask is: 'Did Neety touch anything dirty?'

At this point, Aunty Wendy will lose patience with Nanny. She'll mutter, 'Get a grip on yourself, Mum,' and refuse to answer the question.

Nanny is terrified of germs.

Uncle Mick takes a fat squishy bottle of Tizer out of the fridge as Aunty Wendy glowers at him. He pours some into a glass and then drinks it in one swallow. 'Bloody lovely that is,' he says, banging his glass down into the red washing-up bowl.

'Give me some, give me some, Uncle Mick,' says Effua, displaying the gap between her teeth.

'No. Give some to me,' I say, running up to him and grabbing him round the legs.

Uncle Mick smiles. 'Plenty of water in the tap, girls,' he says. He opens the cupboard over the sink, takes out two plastic beakers and fills them both to the top with lovely, bubbly, orange Tizer. He hands us a beaker each. Nanny has said that only people with 'absolutely no breeding' drink Tizer. But I gulp it down.

'Don't use it all up, Mick,' Aunty Wendy says. 'We've only got one bottle to last us till I go shopping.'

'I might use it all up. I might not,' he says. 'What do you think, Neeta? Will I or won't I?'

He takes a hearty swig from the bottle as I watch him admiringly.

'What we got for tea then, Wendy darling?' says Uncle Mick.

'I thought we'd have fish and chips since it's Saturday. That all right, kids?'

'Might be, might not be,' says Uncle Mick, before Effy or I can answer. He's picking at the wallpaper under the windowsill, where a little bit of it is peeling off.

'I thought you wouldn't mind ridin' your bike down the chippie, my feet are bloody killing me. I don't feel like walking another step.'

'It was your idea to get fish and chips, Wendy, so you'd better bloody well walk down there yourself.'

'Come on, it wouldn't hurt you, love.'

'It won't hurt *you*.'

'You go, Mick. I'm not even hungry am I? Me and the girls had Kentucky for lunch.'

Uncle Mick suddenly takes Aunty Wendy into his arms. 'I was only joking wasn't I?' he says, pressing his thin pink lips against hers and making a squidgy noise. 'What's all that eyeliner muck you got on your eyes then?'

Effua and I stand there, not sure whether to puke or giggle. 'They're in love, aren't they?' I whisper to Effy who just laughs like an idiot.

Without warning, Effy pinches my arm and skips away. I try to catch her and pinch her back but she is far more nimble than me. She appears behind me and pinches me again, on the back of the arm.

'I hate you so much I could die, Effy,' I say.

But I'm fibbing. I love her. Kind of. Grown-ups say we complement each other perfectly, Effy and I. They say that I'm the brains and Effy's the cheek and that we're just like real sisters.

And these are my memories of her. Fighting and giggling. Effy creating mischief, me trying to get her into trouble even on the rare occasion when she hasn't done anything.

And then, on one Saturday that started out just like any other, our sisterhood crashes to a terrifying halt.

'There's some coloured lady just pulled up in a big bloody taxi outside,' Mick says.

'Stop pulling my leg, Mick,' Aunty Wendy says.

A car door slams outside.

'I'm tellin' you,' says Uncle Mick. 'There's some coloured lady gettin' out of a big taxi. Come here and have a bloody look out the window then.'

I'm staying the night at Aunty Wendy's.

As soon as Uncle Mick says the word *coloured*, Effua and I shoot out of her bedroom, where we'd been playing noughts and crosses.

Aunty Wendy's standing by the front door doing nothing, just looking confused. Finally Uncle Mick opens the door and that's when I see Effy's real mother – Aunty Akosua – wriggling out of the taxicab and moving up the garden path like she's dancing at a disco, her bottom rolling and shaking with every step. I look at

Aunty Wendy; Aunty Wendy looks at Uncle Mick. Effua looks at me.

'Long time,' says Aunty Akosua. 'I've come for my daughter.'

'It's a bit late,' Aunty Wendy replies shakily. 'The girls. The girls are about to go to bed.'

'Ama-Effua,' says Aunty Akosua. 'Go an' pack your things.'

'Akosua! They've got school tomorrow,' says Aunty Wendy. Her neck's going pink and her eyes are moving around really fast.

'Pack your things, Effy-baby, it's time for you to come home,' says Aunty Akosua.

'You can't just *take* her,' says Aunty Wendy. 'Mick, tell her she can't just take her.'

Uncle Mick says, 'You'd better come in, I s'pose.'

He closes the door behind her.

Aunty Wendy may have no phone, but news of a coloured foster-girl being snatched travels fast. Within minutes Nanny is at the door, her hair shining bright silver in the moonlight. She dives at me with an astonishing nimbleness and presses me to her until my breath feels trapped inside my chest.

'Oh, darling,' Nanny says. 'Thank God it wasn't you they took. Darling, are you all right?'

'I'm fine, thanks, Nanny.'

'Mr Tucker just rang me up,' she continues, glaring at Aunty Wendy. 'Told me a coloured woman's been here and taken one of the girls with her. I thought someone had taken Anita.'

'But, Mum!' says Aunty Wendy. 'You didn't have to walk all the way over here. Look at you! You're all out of breath!'

'It's just my nerves, stop making a big fuss, for God's sake. And anyway, what was I supposed to do, Wendy? Send a carrier pigeon? It's not my fault you haven't got a phone. This is the last time I'm letting my Nin come out with you. Never again. Not after this. I'm not having my Nin taken from me.'

Nanny's blue mac is buttoned up to her neck and it crackles as she hugs me.

She nods at Uncle Mick who is standing behind Aunty Wendy; he inclines his head slightly in her direction.

'Who's watching Dad?' says Aunty Wendy.

'He's fine on his own for a few minutes. Being on his own for once is hardly going to kill him.'

Nanny grabs my hand. 'It's alright, Nin,' she says. That's her *special* name for me: Nin, short for pickanniny. I hate it. It's dumb. 'Come along, darling. You're safe with your old Nanny. Come on, I'm taking you home.'

'See you later, *Nin*,' says Uncle Mick, chuckling to himself.

No one seems to be aware that all I am wearing are yellow pyjamas with sunflowers on them and a pair of pink fluffy slippers. I blow a kiss bye-bye to Aunty Wendy and Uncle Mick, and then Nanny and I walk, very slowly, to the end of Acacia Way and down West Walk.

'It's very sad, Nin, about Effua, isn't,' says Nanny.

'She's coming back, Nanny.'

Nanny doesn't comment. She just grips my hand tighter.

Miss Biafra

NANNY, GRAMPS AND I live on West Walk, Woodview, behind a bright red door. Our shaggy doormat says WELCOME, which is ironic considering that we discourage visitors and rarely let them in. Knock on our red door out of the blue and we may well turn down our TV and sit in silence behind the net curtains, pretending we're not home, till you mind your own beeswax and bugger off. We only let in social workers – because we have to – and my mother, because she'd kick the door down if we didn't.

On the outside, our house is exactly the same as Aunty Wendy's. We've got the same square-shaped lawn, although the grass on ours is yellowing and not mown as often as hers.

Although we prefer to say 'no' to visitors, our front door's often left on the latch, so that Nanny never has to touch the doorknob. Doorknobs harbour germs. Nanny and I spend a lot of time at Sainsbury's, where Nanny eyes the shelves of germ-killing liquids and disinfectant sprays and then sweeps bottle after bottle of the stuff into our trolley.

It's a miracle that amidst all this fear of germs we have a dog. Judy, the cairn terrier, lives in the cupboard at the bottom of the stairs, where we used to hang our coats. She's imprisoned behind a wooden partition that Uncle Mick installed for us. She never goes out for walks because I'm too young to take her and Nanny's too old. And she's not allowed the run of the house because dogs, Nanny says, are teeming with germs.

I step over the wooden partition, into the dark cupboard and press my face against Judy's fur, inhaling her warm doggy smell. She smells just like a digestive biscuit; I feel like putting one of her tiny sweet little paws into my mouth. If I did, Nanny would scream. I giggle at the thought. Judy looks up at me and licks my face. Nanny watches Judy's tongue on my cheek and shivers with disgust. Ignoring her, I whisper into Judy's fur, 'I love you I love you I love you, Jude.'

'Come on, missy,' says Nanny. 'You need to come and give your hands a good scrub after touching that dog.'

When it comes to germs and germ-eliminating rituals, Nanny is not negotiable. There's no talking your way out of it. In the kitchen, Nanny squirts a minute blob of Jif into my palms to make sure they're squeaky clean. When she finally turns the tap off, Nanny wipes the tap down with a sponge that she's soaked through with Dettol and then scrubs her own hands with Jif, and then again with Ajax. Nanny's hands are red and raw, the skin on them is like one unhealed wound. Watching her hurt herself like this makes me cringe. I also don't want my hands to end up like hers because it looks painful.

Gramps is waiting for us in the sitting room, with his head tipped a little to the side and his eyes half closed. When he tries to say something, his lip hangs down on one side and I can't always follow very easily.

'You were worried sick that Anita had been taken back by her mother, weren't you, Matt?' says Nanny, standing behind Gramps's wheelchair, brushing something off his shoulder.

'Sorry, Gramps,' I say.

Gramps moves his head slightly.

He wasn't always like this. I look up at the framed picture that hangs on our wall behind Gramps's wheelchair. It's Gramps when he was young, wearing his Navy uniform and looking just like Clark Gable, Nanny's favourite film star.

It makes me want to see more pictures of him from when he was a sailor and fought in the war. He travelled all over the world, even to countries where the natives were naked. I think about some of the things that Gramps has seen – headhunters, flying foxes, ladies with no tops on – and wish he could talk to me in a non-disabled language that I could understand. Perhaps he could tell me more about where I came from?

'Nanny? Can I look at the pictures of Gramps and the savages again?' I ask. 'Can I? Please?'

'All right, missy. Run and get me a bit of kitchen towel. That old bureau's filthy.'

Nanny uses the kitchen towel to pull open the bottom drawer of her Victorian writing bureau. As the drawer slides opens a musty odour seeps out. Kneeling, she picks through the smelly old papers in the bottom of the drawer until she finds a thin stack of photographs which she hands to me. I smile up at Gramps who is trying to smile back.

The photographs are very old and they're a cloudy brown like water in a dirty river. I look closely at the first picture; it's of a lady wearing nothing but a skirt that looks like it's made of twigs and leather. She doesn't look even slightly embarrassed about standing there with her bare boobs showing.

In the next picture there are three unsmiling jet-black ladies staring straight ahead, all with short hair that looks like little dots are growing on their round heads. The ladies' bare skin is so shiny that it looks like your hands would just slide all over their bodies if you tried to touch them. I rub my finger along my own arm and then rub the same finger across the photograph.

'They were headhunters, those ladies; every last one of them,' says Nanny.

'How did Gramps meet them?'

'He was stationed in Papua New Guinea just after we got married. He and his men saved some of the natives from getting

27

very ill. Matt sent me one of those pictures as a postcard and I must admit, Nin, I didn't like the thought of him being around those pretty native women, with their boobs all out. I didn't like it one little bit.'

'Do you think those ladies are pretty?' I say.

'Very. Don't you?'

I gaze at the three half-naked ladies. Their shiny noses are just as flat as my nose. Their lips, like mine, are so plump that their mouths look perfectly round even with their lips closed. I don't think they are pretty; I think they look ugly. Like me.

The last picture in the stack of postcards is of a man with a very long beard; a picture I don't remember seeing before.

'His name was Haile Selassie, the King of Abyssinia,' says Nanny. '*Emperor* Haile Selassie. You rescued that emperor on a boat, didn't you, Matt? Gramps saved him from the Italians.'

It seems to me that Gramps, like Jesus, has saved a lot of people.

Eleven or so of us stand in line outside the fire station at the bottom of Woodview, squinting against the sunlight and feeling so worked up and expectant you'd think this was the starting line on Sports' Day. I am in a fancy dress competition; if I win, I will get a five-pound note and a rosette.

Next to me is Weird Mary whose long brown hair is parted down the middle. Mary is wearing a flowery maxi-skirt that looks too big for her and a sash across her chest that has the word PEACE written on it. I'm wearing an orange and black top and wraparound skirt my mother bought me when I was five that now fits me like a sausage skin. Nanny has tied her blue-and-white scarf around my head like a turban and Aunty Wendy's real gold gypsy hoop earrings dangle from my ears. On my wrist there are four sparkly bracelets Uncle Mick found in the lost and found cupboard at work. Over it all is a yellow sash that says MISS BIAFRA.

Nobody but me is dressed up as an African savage.

I wanted to come as Agnetha, the blond lady in ABBA, or as a salamander, in the green-and-yellow velour costume I've seen in the window of the fancy-dress shop in Chichester, but Nanny had other ideas.

'But won't the boys up Herd's Field think I'm a real African, Nanny?' I asked, as Nanny fussed about my head wrap, fixing it with a safety pin. 'Am I a real African, Nanny?'

'What do I always tell you, Nin?' she says. 'You're a British girl, just like everybody else. Don't ever let anybody tell you different.'

'What does Biafra mean?'

'Oh, Biafra was an awful war in Africa, darling. I'll never forget; there was a Biafran woman we read about in the paper who was riding on the train over there, carrying a lovely hatbox. I bet you can't imagine what she had inside the hatbox?'

'No . . .'

'It was her baby's head, darling. The soldiers had cut off the baby's head with a sword.'

I feel like puking up but I also want to hear more. I didn't realise coloured women could love their own children, let alone a mother loving her baby so much that she simply couldn't part with it, even after it was dead. How could Nanny's story be true? All coloured ladies give their babies away for fostering almost as soon as they're born, don't they? Or maybe things are done differently in Africa.

'Where was the rest of the baby's body? Why did the lady only keep the baby's head?'

'I don't know. You do ask some funny questions.'

'Where was the lady going to on the train?'

'Back to her village, I'd think.'

'I didn't know they had trains in Africa.'

'Oh, they do nowadays,' says Nanny. 'I'd think they have all sorts of things going on in Africa that we don't know about.'

*　　　*　　　*

Uncle Mick and the other parents wait a few feet away from us kids in our fancy dress, leaning against the fire station, taking pictures and giving us thumbs-up signs. A few more kids arrive late. Each time a kid in a good costume arrives, Uncle Mick sneers in a way that makes it look like he's got something stuck up his nose.

The very last kid to arrive is Crispin, dressed up as Elvis Presley. Crispin's got a jet-black toupee perched atop his blond hair and there's a real electric guitar strapped across his body.

A man with a gigantic camera tells us all to hold hands and then he walks along inspecting us individually, telling each kid to turn a little to the side or put one hand on their hip before he takes their photograph. To me, he says, 'It wouldn't hurt to smile, sweetheart.'

'What's up with you then, eh?' says Uncle Mick. 'That photographer bloke said you had the best costume and he reckons if you'd a bloody smiled instead of looking so miserable, you'd have come first.'

I've got a rosette pinned to my top that says 2nd and the pound note that I won is curled up in my hand. Uncle Mick and I watch Crispin Boxall, the winner, who is standing with his legs very far apart and pretending to play his guitar while the photographer takes a photo of him that will come out in next week's *Fernmere Observer*.

'Who does that posh little sod think he is?' says Uncle Mick.

As we walk into town, to pick up Aunty Wendy from the hairdresser's where she works, I pull off my MISS BIAFRA sash and slip on the white cardigan that I was wearing tied around my waist. I feel like throwing the sash in the bin.

'Do you think I did any good then, Uncle Mick?' I say, in a very small voice.

'What do you mean, "did any good"?'

'Me coming second in the fancy dress and that.'

'Yeah,' he says. 'Coming second is about as good as coming last.'

We walk along Pudding Row in silence.

'For Christ's sake, cheer up, misery guts,' says Uncle Mick. 'Far as I'm concerned, you was the best in the whole bloody competition.'

Nanny says it does Gramps's heart good to see me dressed in African gear. And it's true. When my picture's printed in the *Fernmere Observer*, a week later, Gramps smiles proudly and tries to clap his hands.

The King Is Dead

WE HAVE ANOTHER BIAFRAN in our house now; my mysterious so-called half-sister Agnes who arrived in 1975. She sleeps here but doesn't seem to be part of our family.

I was up at my mother's one weekend when Mummy Elizabeth rang Nanny and instructed her to drive to Haslemere station. When Nanny and Aunty Wendy arrived, there was me, there was Mummy Elizabeth – and then there was this girl-woman, who I'd thought was my Aunty Agnes. She was standing there bare-legged and shivering in a cotton party dress, carrying a bloated suitcase. She'd been in England three and a half days.

I'd been told, to start with, that Agnes was my aunty, my mother's baby sister. But once we all got to Nanny's house, my mother's story changed.

'Agnes is my first child. Anita's senior sister,' Mummy Elizabeth said, as casually as if she was reading out a grocery list.

None of us said anything. Previously my mother had claimed that I was an only child and that I probably always would be. So how could I possibly have a sister?

'Agnes's going to attend Fernmere Grammar School,' Mummy Elizabeth said.

'How lovely,' said Nanny, warily. 'Where's she going to stay?'
'Here.'
'Where?'
'She's moving in here with you and Anita, right away,' said my

mother. 'Agnes! Stop standing there like an idiot! Come inside and introduce yourself.'

'But,' said Nanny. 'But, Lizzy, I don't know her. I don't have the room.'

Nanny had no choice but to take Agnes in. Had she refused, Mummy Elizabeth was going to pack my bags and 'remove' me from Nanny straight away. She'd send me and this Agnes off to some other foster home. Nanny told my mother she'd certainly need more 'keep' if there were going to be two girls under her roof – what with one of them almost fully grown. Mummy Elizabeth stood up, raised her voice, said she was really going to have to find somebody whose rates were more reasonable, and told Agnes to 'go upstairs and pack Anita's bags'.

Nanny began clenching and unclenching her little fists. Mummy Elizabeth told Nanny she'd have to spread the money she received for me between the two of us newfound sisters. Nanny's face suddenly glowed like one of the fake embers on our electric fire. She kicked at the carpet with her poorly, water-inflated right foot, and then she caved in.

We borrowed Aunty Wendy's folding bed, cleared my toys into a huge box and set Agnes up in the box room, which was sandwiched between Nanny's bedroom and the staircase. Later, when Agnes was shut inside the box room, sobbing, Nanny told me she'd rather go bankrupt than have me taken away from her. That the only way I could ever be taken from her was over her dead body.

I asked Nanny, 'Is Agnes really my sister?'

'I don't blinking know, Nin. Her skin's a lot darker than yours, darling, and she seems ever so African in her ways.'

'Aggy the nigger lion' is what the kids at Fernmere Grammar School call this new sister of mine. In Biology, she says, they ask her if her blood comes out black. On the rare occasion that

Agnes speaks to me, she pulls me into the tiny box room and fills me in on the 'racialist' names she's been called that day.

'I bet nobody's ever called you a Nigger Lion, little miss perfect,' she says, holding me by the elbow, forcing me to face her so I can't escape the impact of the words. She sounds almost triumphant, like she's desperate for me to know, to experience, how much she is suffering.

Nanny says Agnes and I don't see eye to eye. That Agnes is jealous of me and that it was unfair on Agnes to prise her away from her own people back in Africa, where she lived happily with my mother's mother and father.

To me, Aggy is the grooviest-looking person I've ever seen – that Fernmere has ever seen – apart from on TV. She looks cool, like those coloured girls you see in flares and midriff-baring halter-neck tops, getting on down in the audience on *Top of the Pops*, glistening with sweat and hair-grease.

Despite our hushed conversations in the box room Aggy doesn't seem to like me much. The first proper conversation we ever had went like this: 'Look at how you act, Anita! Listen to how you talk! You think you are white!'

'So what? At least I'm not an African cannibal like you!'

Two years after all this happened, Aggy's still reluctantly living with us.

'Run upstairs and see if that sulky bitch Agnes is in her room for me, will you?' says Nanny.

I tear up the stairs and knock on the door to the box room. I press my ear against the wood. No response. I knock again. Silence. Agnes is very light on her feet and can slip down the stairs and through our front door without being heard; she could be anywhere. I envy her freedom. She may be out eating ice-cream or drinking Pepsi in a café – or, for all we know, she's smoking fags in the bus shelter.

Or perhaps she's gone round to Aunty Wendy's for one of her

showers. Agnes goes there nearly every day now because Nanny finds it impossible to let anyone touch her bathroom unless she's right in there, supervising them. Agnes demands privacy and claims she needs to wash her body every day. She calls the shower a 'bath' and she pronounces it 'batt'. It's like a ritual. She uses a special bundle of beige fibrous twigs that Mummy Elizabeth gives her, to clean her skin.

'Aggy's not in there, Nanny!' I shout from the landing.

The phone rings downstairs and I tiptoe down to eavesdrop. I hear Nanny speaking in her special phone voice. The very posh voice where it sounds almost like she's singing; or reading the *Nine O' Clock News*.

'Oh, but Lizzy!' sings Nanny. 'My Wendy was planning on taking Neety to the Isle of Wight this weekend.'

I am horrified to hear that it's Mummy Elizabeth. I feel my familiar world collapsing in on me.

'Nin! It's your mother on the telephone! Neety – it's for yoo-hoo!'

Nanny opens the sitting-room door, which nearly smacks me in the face.

'Good God,' says Nanny. 'You almost made me jump out of my skin. What are you hiding behind the door for, my little pickanniny?'

'I'm not speaking to her,' I whisper, afraid Mummy Elizabeth might hear me and reach through the phone and get me.

Nanny had told me that my mother was in Africa again. One of her relatives had died. She didn't tell me which one. It's been months and months since I've seen my mother and I've started pretending she doesn't exist. I told my friend Becky at school that my mother died, that I'm an orphan.

'Do I *have* to speak to her, Nanny?'

'Neety, you know you have to speak to your mother. Now stop being silly and take this phone.'

Nanny wipes our phone with kitchen towel smothered with Jif, leaving a powdery residue on the receiver. Gramps is in his wheelchair with his eyes closed. I wish I was him. No one forces him to speak to people he hates on the phone.

'NITTY? Is that you, Nitty?' screams Mummy Elizabeth.

Who on earth does she think it is? Of course it's me. Hearing my mother's heavily accented voice fills me with dread. I don't want this weird, unkind, loud, constantly disappearing woman to be my mother. I feel pinpricks of tears forming behind my eyes.

'It's me,' I force myself to say.

'Nitty!'

'Yes, mother?'

'Nitty, darling, it's your mummy!'

Does she think I'm three years old or something?

'I'm back in London, Nitty.'

I hate being called Nitty. Why can't she pronounce it Neety, the way everyone else does? Nitty just makes me think of the nit comb at school and the scalding humiliation I feel when Mrs West, the school nurse, calls my hair 'woolly' and complains that she can't get the nit comb through 'hair like this'.

'How are you, darling?'

'I'm fine, thank you.' Nanny's taught me to always say that when someone asks. Regardless of whether I'm fine or not.

Nanny nods now, showing me I've said the right thing. She's standing next to me, rubbing her hands together again and again.

'Tell your mother you've been ill with a nasty cold and a sore throat,' Nanny instructs.

'I've been ill with a nasty cold and throat,' I mumble.

'Oh, sorry, darling! Is your throat still painin' you?'

'No.'

'Tell her it was probably the change in the weather that did it,' says Nanny.

'It was the change in the weather that gave me the cold.' I say dutifully.

'Tell your mother you've nearly grown out of your school uniform.'

'Tell Nanny to stop telling you what to say,' says Mummy Elizabeth. 'Tell Nanny to just shut up.' She pronounces this 'shot up'.

'I can't. I'm not allowed.'

'What? Hold on, OK. Your aunty wants to talk to you.'

'Anita!' screeches this nameless aunty. 'Do you know who this is?'

'No.'

'This is your Aunty Onyi!'

'Wow! Hi, Aunty Onyi.'

I had feared Aunty Onyi, my mother's baby sister, was the relative who'd apparently died in Nigeria last year. Aunty Onyi's the only coloured grown-up I've ever met who I liked. She is giggly, has an American accent and two-inch-long red nails.

'Anita, we're having a party tonight and I'd like you to come,' says Aunty Onyi. 'We're celebrating my graduation.'

My mother comes back on the phone. 'We'll come and pick you up later, Nitty.'

'What does graduation mean, mother?' I ask.

I hear the paper boy drop our *Daily Mirror* through the letter-box. Judy barks loudly.

'What is that sound?' says my mother. 'It sounds like a dog barking.'

'It's Judy.'

I see Nanny shaking her head and mouthing the word 'no'.

'Give me Nanny,' says my mother.

I hand Nanny the receiver.

'It's not *our* dog,' Nanny says, smirking. 'We're just looking after it, for our next-door neighbours. They're . . . on holiday. All right, I'll put Neety back on.'

'Stupid white people, and these disgusting animals crawling everywhere,' moans Mother.

'Sorry, Mother.'

'It is not your fault, darling. Now, Nitty. Tell me, how is Agnes?'

I shrug.

'Are you deaf?' my mother shouts. 'I asked you, "how is Agnes?" Give me Nanny again.'

Nanny tells Mother that Aggy's gone out. Then she says, 'All right. Yes, all right. Yes, we'll be expecting you.'

Nanny puts the phone down and hurries into the kitchen to wash her hands. I follow her and hold out my own hands obediently so that she can massage a squirt of Fairy liquid into them and then rinse the germs from the phone safely down the plughole.

'Your mother told me she wants our Judy destroyed. Arrogant bloody bitch. Thinks she can tell me what to do in my own house.'

I feel light-headed with fear at the thought of my mother breaking into our house in the night and killing Judy. 'Can I have a Wagon Wheel please Nanny?' I turn to food, the way I always do when I am afraid.

'Help yourself to a bit of kitchen towel and use it to open the cabinet and take one. Make sure you don't get your dirty little mitts all over the inside of my cabinet, Nin, won't you?'

When I amble back into the kitchen having eaten three Wagon Wheels, Nanny is still washing her hands and she looks deep in thought. I open the kitchen bin to toss in the contaminated piece of kitchen towel.

'Nin, don't you dare touch the lid of that bin with your hands!'

'Are we going to be allowed to keep Judy?' My voice comes out high and thin like Donna Summers'.

'I don't know, Nin. I don't know.'

Nanny sends me to my room to write a short story to read out to her after our tea. 'You know how I love to hear your stories,' she says.

I will write a story about my mother, designed to make Nanny and Gramps laugh – or shudder.

I sit at my dressing table with a blank writing pad in front of me, staring at my reflection in the three-way mirror. I'm shocked once again at how ugly I look. My lips are as fat as satsuma slices and my nose so flat it looks like I got hit with a hammer.

I look away in disgust and gaze instead at the state of my room. Nanny's going to go spare when she sees it. She boasts constantly about how neat and tidy I am. My shiny pink eiderdown is draped across the floor, where I left it after I used it earlier as a cloak when I dressed up and pretended to be a queen. There are piles of books all around my bed. *101 Dalmations*. *James and the Giant Peach*. A Collins Gem dictionary. Nanny's BT phone book. *Little Red Riding Hood*. *Grimm's Illustrated Fairy Tales*.

'Once upon a time . . .' I write in my exercise book. 'There was a lady called Lizzy who was . . .'

Who was what? I don't know anything much about my mother, do I?

I close my eyes and think of all the stories inside my huge stash of overdue library books. I picture my mother as Cruella de Vil and I see her parading into our sitting room, lips shining with the blood of freshly killed cairn terrier puppies.

And then I hear a whoosh of crackly music, coming from the box room.

I sprint along the hall and rap on the door again and again. No answer. I turn the handle and peer in to the semi-darkness of an un-aired room. There's a smell of singed hair and Charlie perfume.

'Excuse me, madam,' I say, copying words I've heard Nanny use. 'But would you mind terribly turning this racket down? You're ruining my short story.'

'Come here, you cheeky little monkey,' says Agnes. She drags me by the arm further into the darkness. Her curtains are shut as usual, just as they are all day and all night.

'Why did you pretend to not be in just now?' I say.

Agnes ignores my question and sits me down on the bed and

39

stands in front of me, hands on hips. She's wearing a white polo neck and bell-bottom jeans that make her thighs look massive. Her hair is in the umbrella style. She flips a 7-inch on to her dusty jumble-sale record player and a man begins singing 'Love Me Tender' in a horrid slow-motion voice and she begins to dance, slowly swaying her round hips and slim shoulders. She clicks her fingers right in my face and laughs.

We don't know exactly how old Agnes really is (Mummy Elizabeth's given us two completely different years of birth for her) but she's definitely in her teens and *should* be studying hard for her CSEs. Instead she puts all her energy into disco dancing and has become the most accomplished dancer in the whole of Fernmere.

I'd love Agnes to teach me to disco dance, but even if she wanted to, there's no room for two of us to dance at the same time in the box room. My own bedroom's big enough for us to practise in together but Agnes's not allowed in my room. Nanny says she's got orders from Mummy Elizabeth that too much 'mixing' with Agnes is banned because it might taint the way I speak and make me sound African. After all, what would be the point of giving your daughter the advantage of speaking and acting white if only to have it all undermined and Africanised? Later my mother will claim it was Nanny who had banned Agnes from my bedroom for fear of me becoming 'a full-blown African'.

There's a new poster on Agnes's wall, above her bed.

'Who's that in the poster?'

'David Essex, you spac.'

'Who's he?'

Agnes gives me her you-have-to-be-kidding look.

'What have you been doing in here all day?' I say.

'Today is a terrible day-O,' Agnes says.

'How come? Is it because Mother's coming?'

'Who told you she's finally bothering to come down? Nanny?'

I nod. Agnes grimaces and moves about her tiny room impatiently, like a caged lion. 'What's wrong with your hair?' she asks suddenly. 'You look like a hedgehog. You look like you've had an electric shock.'

'No I don't.'

'You bloomin' do.'

'Agnes. Can I ask you a question?'

'Of course.'

'Is our mother really our mother?'

'Of course she is. How can you ask me that? You look just like her.'

'I do not!'

'You do. You should be proud. She's pretty.'

'She's disgusting,' I say. 'Agnes, if we're really sisters, then how come we haven't got the same dad?'

'Because I've got my own dad. You've got your own dad.'

I've never owned any picture of my dad. If he's real, if I really have a dad, how come I've never heard his voice or got a postcard from him? I suspect my dad, whoever he is, dropped dead years ago and that nobody's telling me about it because they think I'm too young to know.

It's all right for Agnes. She's got a dad back in Nigeria. Her dad's name is Sunday, I think. She looks like him. I've seen a picture of him in her room. He's got a massive nose, like her.

'What has got into you today?' says Agnes. 'Leave me with this nonsense. I'm grievin' today, isn't it?'

'What's wrong with you?'

'The King died today.'

'What king?'

'Elvis. He was *only* the greatest musician of all time. Sad, innit?'

'Nope. It's not sad.'

'You little devil.'

Agnes playfully pulls my hair. Almost certainly some of my

41

hair will snap off in her hand. I have unbelievably terrible hair. It's tough enough to break most combs that have ever been used on it, but at the same time loads of my hair breaks off every time you try to comb it.

'Come here,' says Agnes. 'Let's see if we can do the umbrella style on you before our mother arrives.'

The umbrella style is Afro hair made smooth as silk with a hot comb then curled in to an exaggerated flip using curling tongs. Agnes plugs in her curling tong and rubs a big turquoise dollop of Ultra Sheen into my scalp and sprays Sta Sof Fro into my hair – and eyes.

It's teatime. Nanny sits opposite me, watching me eat a banana and sugar sandwich made with bread as white and soft as cotton wool. My lips are covered with sugar and butter.

The bright white kitchen table is set just for me. Nanny's got no appetite because she's sad I'm leaving her for the weekend. Agnes has gone to her job at the nursing home where she spends the evening wiping old people's bums.

Earlier, I heard Nanny tell Mummy Elizabeth that Agnes had to leave for work at six.

'I'll be there by five thirty at the latest,' my mother said.

It is now half past seven.

'What do you think my mother will be like now?' I say.

'Adults don't change, darling. That woman will still be tall and ever so high-faluting, I would think.'

'Do you think she'll be nice this time?'

'How would I know, darling?'

Nanny covers my hand with hers. There are little bits of dry skin flaking off her hand like white confetti.

'I know you don't want to go to your mum, but it's only for the weekend. You *know* there's nothing I can do to stop her making you go up to London with her. She's your mother.'

'I know, Nanny. I love you.'

'And I love you too, darling. You know that, don't you, darling?'

Judy begins barking. There is the sound of a cuckoo hooting at the front door. The cuckoo is Aunty Wendy who makes that noise every time she comes round. To let us know it's her before she nudges our front door open.

'All right, Mum?' she says, sitting down at the table, stretching out her toes. 'All right, Neet?'

Aunty Wendy's carrying a handbag my mother brought her from Africa last year. It's made from a lizard's skin. She's also wearing the shoes she normally saves for very special occasions: gold flip-flops she got from Woolworth's in Chichester.

'You hear anything back yet from your letter to little Effy?' says Nanny.

'Not a thing. Been ringing and ringing her mother's number as well from the phone box. No one ever answers,' says Aunty Wendy.

I feel angry at once on so many levels: because Aunty Wendy has done herself up just for Mummy Elizabeth, and acts like my mother's a visiting dignitary. And with Effy, for leaving me, even though I know she had no choice in the matter. I don't understand why it's taking her so long to find her way back.

'Is this it then, for my tea?' I snap, hoping that I sound every bit as rude as Uncle Mick. That'll give Nanny and Aunty Wendy something to think about. 'Is this all I'm getting?'

'Are you gonna let her get away with talking to you like that, Mum?' says Aunty Wendy.

We're interrupted by the soft gurgle of my mother's car outside our open sitting-room window, then the jingle of car keys. I have not forgotten the sound the leather soles of my mother's Italian shoes make as they scuff against the concrete of our garden path. Today, as usual, there are also other footsteps approaching our house too; the scrape, scrape of high heels and a solid, flat-footed plod.

Suddenly I'm almost desperate to see my mother and for her

to see me. Since she last met me I've grown a lot taller and I won an award for one of my poems at school. My hair, though still awful, has grown longer too, and thanks to Agnes it is stiff and shining. I am eager for Mummy Elizabeth to be forced to swallow her own words and admit that I'm not that dull, I'm not as boring as she's made out.

Nanny and Wendy rise from their chairs and stand at attention.

Pathetic! I think. Grown-ups actually straighten their backs and speak more slowly and crisply whenever Mummy Elizabeth is in close proximity. Everyone seems afraid of my mother, even her own sisters. Even me. Especially me. I suck in my tummy, hold my breath, pull my shoulders back. If only I had the courage to stick out my tongue at her and show her two fingers.

'The door's open!' says Nanny.

My mother has proudly described herself to me before as 'anti-social'. Hardly. Even if she is rude all the time to almost all people, she always has friends and family members swarming around her with smiling faces and terrified eyes.

Mummy Elizabeth advances into our kitchen, closely followed by a very round plump baby-faced lady and a very thin male stranger. She is wearing black sunglasses and a white suit covered in tiny navy blue polka dots. My mother never, ever, wears the African clothes you might expect her to wear. She once told me 'African garb' is for people who are 'primitive and unsophisticated'. My mother's clothes are made on the Continent, by white people. But the plump lady and the thin man are done up in African gear, which swishes crisply as they move; all of it brightly coloured, like sweet wrappers.

'Hallo, you *do* look well, Lizzy,' Nanny says. 'How was the traffic?'

Hallo, you do look well, I hiss under my breath.

'Nitty,' my mother says, removing her dark glasses and staring at me like I'm a statue in a museum. I really, really hate being stared at. I'm afraid people can see right inside me and steal my thoughts.

It seems my mother's waiting for me to say something and I can't think of anything to say. I think hard.

'What time is it in London, Mother?' I say, finally.

She winks at me. I try to wink back but I can't close one eye at a time and so I just blink. She giggles and blinks back at me. What on earth is going on? Since when did Mummy Elizabeth smile or giggle? What's happened to her since she came back from Nigeria?

'How you been keeping?' asks Aunty Wendy.

'Fine,' says my mother.

'How's your old mum, in Africa?' says Nanny. 'You said she hasn't been too well.'

'She's fine.'

My mother glances through our kitchen window into our wild back garden. She props up her chin with the spiky knuckle of her hand and stacks up evil thoughts.

'Come into the sitting room, everyone,' says Nanny quickly.

The thin man, who my mother introduces as Mr Obinna, tries to get his hands on my hair.

'What is this?' he says. 'Dreadlocks or something? Jamo-style?'

Before he can get at my hair with some hidden Afro comb I leap away from him and run to Nanny's side.

'Neety!' he says. 'You've really grown!'

I want to ask this Mr Obinna when he has ever seen me before, but I can't get a word in because suddenly our sitting room is filled with many different voices, all speaking at once.

'Anita, I am so excited to see you!' cries Aunty Onyi.

'Why?' I say, and blush.

Aunty Wendy walks over and puts an arm around me and says, 'Don't your hair look nice, Neet?'

'Her hair is *terrible*,' my mother says. 'Where is Agnes? She should be doing a better job with Anita's hair.'

'Wendy and I have tried to put her hair into plaits, the way you do it, Lizzy,' says Nanny. 'But we can't manage it, can we Wendy?

I don't think our fingers are as nimble as yours. We love it in that melon style you do.'

What a traitor Nanny is in front of my mother. When my mother has done the melon style – a series of plaits woven in lines close to my head and ending in a braided bun pulled together so tightly that your eyes can't help but slant – on me in the past, Nanny's been there with a knitting needle as soon as my mother's left, unpicking the plaits for me because they're too tight and they hurt.

'Oh, don't make a face, Anita,' Nanny says. 'You look absolutely beautiful when your hair's done like that. It makes you look just like that darling little pickaninny Topsy.'

Nanny's always comparing me to Topsy. Topsy is a little coloured girl, a character in Nanny's favourite-ever book, *Uncle Tom's Cabin*. Like me, Topsy doesn't have a proper mother or father and her past is a puzzle no one can solve. It was reading *Uncle Tom's Cabin* when she was a little girl that's made Nanny fall head-over-heels in love with coloured people; especially coloured children. I wonder whether Mummy Elizabeth has read, or heard of, *Uncle Tom's Cabin*.

Mr Obinna says, 'You don't remember me, hey Anita?'

'No.'

'So rude!' complains my mother. 'This is Mr Obinna, your uncle.'

Mr Obinna's blue-and-gold cap is glinting now in the sudden sunlight that's pouring through the sitting-room window.

'What a lovely hat,' Nanny says. She can't pronounce the man's name, so she calls him Sir. 'What a lovely hat, Sir. Is it a fez? Reminds me of that wonderful hat Tommy Cooper wears.'

Mr Obinna smiles in a supercilious fashion, the exact way coloured people always seem to smile at Nanny.

'So, Anita, do you know who you are?' he says, turning back to me.

'Yes. I am Anita Williams. *Precious* Anita Williams.'

'But do you know that you're Igbo? Do you know who your *people* are?' he says. 'Your people are a royal family you know. Let me tell you the story,' Mr Obinna continues, 'First, were the Uche. Five brothers. All called Uche.'

Just as I'm getting interested in hearing the story, he stops and sits there looking blankly at me.

'What happened next?' I ask.

I notice that unless I say, 'Gosh' or, 'Wow! Really uncle?' after every three or four words he utters, Mr Obinna will stop the story.

'There was King Eze Uche,' he continues. 'There was Obinna Uche. Hold on a minute, aren't you going to write this down, Anita? I thought I heard you liked writing stories. Take this down; U-C-H-E. U for onion, C for cat . . .'

'Isn't onion spelled with an O?' I say, drawing a sunflower in the little notepad I always carry in my pocket. My mother glares at me.

'H for heaven, E for egg,' says Mr Obinna. 'There were five of the Uche brothers and King Eze Uche, your great-grandfather, was the oldest and the richest.'

'What a wonderful story,' says Nanny.

I scribble 'The Africans are real weirdos' in my notepad.

'Your grandfather too, was a celebrated man,' says Mr Obinna. 'He was one of the first Nigerian millionaires. He was a millionaire in US dollars, not only in *naira*.'

My mother's mouth splits into a smile. Even Gramps smiles.

'He was a very powerful, very rich man,' my mother says. 'He would put money on to the ground and tell me to dance on top of the money. Nitty, we have to get going. Your uncle can tell you the rest of the story in the car.'

My mother leads me by the arm out into the hall where Judy is howling.

'That dog had better be removed before I return Anita,' she says, 'If it's not gone, I'll remove the damned thing myself.'

When I Had You To Myself

MY MOTHER'S CAR SMELLS of oranges. And unlike Nanny's ancient Datsun, this car's floor is carpeted, in cream, and it's not littered with empty crisp packets, Ribena cartons and sweet wrappers.

Mummy Elizabeth presses buttons and things instantly happen: the doors lock, the windows roll up, the space suddenly fills up with music – Donna Summer's voice singing the song 'I Feel Love'. One of the slippery pale leather seats juts backwards. This, I imagine, is how it would feel to be inside a spaceship.

I can see Nanny and Aunty Wendy standing next to Gramps's wheelchair through the sitting room window. They grow smaller and smaller until we turn the bend out of sight. I feel a deep sense of dread. This spaceship, even though it has cuddly, giggly Aunty Onyi in it, is surely delivering me, at top speed, straight to hell.

'Look at her face!' says my mother, who has been watching me in her mirror.

'What you crying for, darling?' says Aunty Onyi.

'She's crying for her white nanny,' says my mother. 'Bloody Nanny.'

'You love your white nanny, Anita?' says Mr Obinna.

I nod. 'Yes. I love Nanny and she loves me.'

There's laughter.

My mother shakes her head. 'They're sick, sick people,' she says. 'That woman. Nanny. Always kissing Anita on the lips.'

*   *   *

Aunty Onyi, who is sitting next to me in the back, hands me a Caramac bar. Aunty Onyi, who hasn't seen me for at least two years, has remembered that I crave sweets. She cares about little details like that, probably because she must spend so much time dreaming about becoming a mother and fantasising about all the wonderful little things she would do for her child if only she could have one of her own.

I cram a piece of the squishy sweet caramel into my mouth as I listen to more of Mr Obinna's story and gradually I give myself over to the tale. I start to feel like I am actually in Africa with this King Eze Uche bloke, marching through something called the Evil Forest. Giving people orders and wading through piles and piles of money.

'The people in the village would follow him just for a chance to smell his farts,' says Mr Obinna.

I laugh so hard that some of the Caramac, now melting, oozes down to my chin.

My mother's head swivels round to face me, her lips pursed and crossed. 'This is not funny, Anita,' she says. 'This is real.'

'How come you didn't want to stay in Africa?' I ask quietly.

I know that my mother came from Nigeria but she's never made it clear why she fled the place, or why she left Agnes – who must have been a baby then – behind. Now, just like that, she begins to unravel a portion of the mystery of her past.

My mother says she used to work for the Bank of America in Lagos. She loved her job and was chased all over the city by important men who wanted to marry her. Agnes stayed with Mother's grandparents in their village.

While still at the Bank of America, my mother fancied a change. She signed up to become one of Nigeria's first-ever air hostesses, flying for Air Nigeria. The novelty wore off quickly: maybe she didn't like having to take orders and serve people drinks and food. After working on a flight that brought her to

England, my mother instantly resigned from air hostessing and remained in London. She bought a house.

She was strolling down Oxford Street one morning when a white man in a raincoat began following her. She stopped, turned and said 'Can I help you?' and he told her she had the most amazing legs he had ever seen, that he was a photographer and that she had what it took to be a fashion model.

Mother took the man's advice and became a model, but she had to give up modelling once she fell pregnant with me. So she began working for a lawyer named Mishcon, who went on to become Baron Mishcon, the QC.

'Are you a lawyer too, Mummy?'

'No,' she snaps. 'I was just extraordinarily good with figures.'

So good was my mother with figures that she used to scare Mr Mishcon because he would reel off clients' names to her and she would be able to tell him off the top of her head the exact amount that was on any client's ledger at that precise moment in time. Mr Mishcon nicknamed her 'Figures'.

'Anita, listen,' my mother cries. 'You need to learn about my grandfather. My grandfather was very, very powerful. He accumulated so much money! Before the white expatriates had telephones, he had a telephone in his house. And this was years ago. In the 1920s.'

Aunty Wendy and Uncle Mick don't have a phone in their house even now and it's the 1970s. Nor do half the people on Woodview.

'He was judge, lawyer and king,' says my mother.

'So was he like Mr Mishcon?'

'No. He was much more important. He was carried around in an *amok*. Do you know what an *amok* is?'

'No, Mother'

'It's like the thing the Roman slaves carried their kings in,' says Aunty Onyi. 'Isn't it?'

My mother ignores her sister and continues.

'A book was published about him too, in the 1930s. It's called *Anayo* and it was the first ever fiction to be written down in Igbo. Except it's not a fiction. They call the hero of the book Anayo, but the book is really about Eze Uche, my grandfather.'

'Wow!' I say. 'What does he do in the book?'

'It's about his life, isn't it? How the whites made him into a king and how he became rich and then lost a lot of money and then became incredibly rich again.'

'Have you got it at your house, mother? The book about him?'

'No.'

I have never seen any books in any of my mother's houses. All I have seen there is the *Daily Mirror* and an amazing magazine called *Ebony*, which is full of pictures of long-haired ladies who look like Sindy dolls, except their skins are beige, bronze or cinnamon-coloured instead of white.

'Anyway,' my mother says. 'You wouldn't be able to understand the book. It's written in Igbo. They've got it at home, in Aro-Eze.'

'What did your grandfather look like, mother?'

'He was very black. Very short. Barely even five feet tall. But he was so powerful that all the other men wished they could look just like him. He turned his short stature into an asset.'

I look down at my feet which are long and narrow in my sandals, indicating that I will one day become tall and narrow just like my mother.

'Why are you so tall then, mother? If your grandfather's so little?'

'My dad was six foot six. It's amazing my dad was able to grow so tall considering the fright he got when his own dad sold him.'

'Why did his dad sell him?'

'Because he wouldn't go to school,' she says matter-of-factly. 'My dad used to climb up a mango tree on the way to school and hang out in the forest all day. His dad was spending a lot of money sending him to school but he wasted that money by not going.

He was very mischievous. So, my dad's younger brother told on him and one day my grandfather followed him and caught him up the mango tree. And he sold him.'

I think about my grandfather being sold, and a door of hope opens inside me. Maybe my mother got rid of me simply because I was very naughty. Like my grandfather. Maybe I *wasn't* born an evil unwant-able spirit. Except of course my mother didn't sell me; she pays Nanny to look after me.

'What are you making a face for?' Mummy Elizabeth says. 'Children were sold off then and no one batted an eyelid. People didn't get all sentimental about children the way white people do. You have to understand, Nitty. Men had so many wives then and they had so many children then. It didn't make that much difference if one of them got sent away.

'But my grandmother was quite angry about my dad being sold because he was her favourite son. And luckily she was a very powerful woman; she came from a rich family. What a formid-able woman! Oh, believe me – when she sang, she could wake up the dead! She had a very powerful voice.'

The dead in Nigeria are always waking up. When somebody dies there, they only seem to die for a little while, a few years at most. Then they come back. A grandchild or nephew is born and the dead person's spirit enters the newborn's body. I've been told I am the living image of one of my great-aunts; a woman with a delicate constitution who wept like a child every time she saw anyone or anything – even a tiny insect – hurt.

'So what happened to your dad in the end, Mummy?'

'My grandmother ran to find the people her husband had sold my dad to and she paid them double the money they'd already paid for him and she got him back. Then she ran off back to her own family with my dad – leaving her husband and the rest of her children behind. She never came back to my grandfather's home until she was dead. Her last wish was to be buried behind my grandfather's big house in Aro-Eze; and that is where she is

52

buried. But her grave is only marked by a palm tree. So the rain is beating her. *Beating her!'*

Despite his penchant for selling children (or perhaps *because* of it), my mother says she had great respect for her grandfather, the King. My mother's English name was given to her by her mother and inspired by the scary, ghost-faced Queen Elizabeth the 1st, but it was my mother's grandfather who suggested her Nigerian name: Oluchi. Meaning 'God's creation'.

As we cruise out of Sussex and then through the last traces of Surrey; as glistening foliage gives way to the motorway and stark concrete: I come to a realisation. I had imagined that I now despised my mother but here, in her presence, that layer of hatred around my heart proves to be flimsy. It is unravelling easily.

All the way to London, my mother's fantastic stories continue to flow out of her like an enchanted river. Aunty Onyi and Mr Obinna keep quiet, just listening and occasionally nodding.

I hear that my great-grandfather had thirty-six wives and more than two hundred and fifty children. I'm told that in Aro-Eze, where my great-grandfather lived, me, Agnes, my mother and Aunty Onyi and Aunty Adaeze are all considered princesses.

'But would they actually *call* me Princess?' I ask.

My mother turns her head my way and blinks her eyes at me.

'*Would* they, mother?'

No answer.

I sit there feeling as though I'm not in a car at all but rather floating above the earth in a dream-scape, bloated with all this new information and drunk with the thrill of finally knowing a chunk of my history. A princess! It almost makes sense. I have been accused before of being aloof and since I've looked the word up in my dictionary, I know that aloof means that I 'hold myself apart from others'. Such behaviour is surely fitting for a princess, I think.

But the only princesses I know of are Princess Anne, Princess Margaret and Cinderella. I didn't realise you could get coloured princesses or that princesses could be foster-children.

'Mama?' I say and I have not called Mummy Elizabeth Mama since I was about three years old. But now I'm beginning to love her again and the word just slips out. 'Please can I ask you a question? If I'm really a princess, how come I live on a council estate?'

'Never stop asking questions, do you?' my mother says, flicking amused eyes across my face then turning her eyes back to the road ahead.

We arrive at my mother's new flat, where her big sister Aunty Adaeze is waiting, lounging on a sofa, dressed in a gold African outfit. Aunty Adaeze is thinner and less jovial than Aunty Onyi, but she has the same kind of face: shaped like a pumpkin with cheeks you just want to pinch and dark eyes barely bigger than slits.

'What do you think of your mummy's new flat?' Aunty Adaeze says.

'It's fine,' I say.

Everything is shiny and the colour of vanilla ice cream, from the weird slippery sofa to the smooth chunky dining table. There are no carpets; your footsteps echo when you walk across the smooth shiny floors.

We all sit down on the sofa in a room my mother calls 'the parlour'. The sofas are so new that the see-through plastic is still on them and we keep sliding towards the edge of the seat. Four pairs of expectant African eyes are focused entirely on me. I can think of absolutely nothing to say.

'Precious!' says Aunty Onyi, pinching my cheek and moving it from side to side.

'Precious Anita!' says Aunty Adaeze.

Why do my aunties get so excited just from saying my name?

'Anita, you're so tall! You look just like your mother, eh?'

'Do I, Aunty?'

'You have your mother's stature.'

'What's a stature?'

Aunty Onyi laughs and then says, again, 'Precious Anita!'

'Where's the picture?' says Aunty Adaeze

'Go and get the picture,' says Aunty Onyi

My mother slips into her bedroom and comes back holding a photograph in a gold frame, a photograph that she has shown me before. It's of a girl with long, dusty-looking brown legs, in a very short white skirt and a white jacket so tight that it looks like her chest will explode. It is my mother as a girl. When she still lived in Africa.

'See?' says Aunty Onyi. 'Your mother was modelling!'

I look at my mother's image and my eyes linger on her hair, which is straight and shiny and hangs almost to her waist in the photo.

'That was a wig,' says Aunty Adaeze.

My mother sucks her teeth and makes no comment.

In the picture, my mother is pouting, just like she is now. I can't see whether she had the gap between her teeth back then, or not. This must have been her when she was working for the Bank of America. I'm not surprised that a country as glamorous as America would hire somebody like her to represent their bank.

My mother has brought me a new outfit which she hands to me in an Army & Navy carrier bag. The outfit has that new clothes smell: a slight undercurrent of chemicals behind the fresh fabric. I wriggle into it while standing behind my mother, looking over her head into the huge gold mirror on her dressing table. I'm astonished and excited my mother has bought me new gear, but I don't think she realised how much I've grown. My new bell-bottom jeans don't reach anywhere near my ankles and the pale-pink and shocking-pink striped T-shirt ends above my belly button.

But Mummy Elizabeth doesn't appear to notice there's a problem.

'Turn around,' she says. 'Turn back around. It suits you, Nitty!'

She is sitting at her dressing table, flicking a toothpick in between the teeth at the back of her mouth. Tossing the toothpick into the bin, she takes a gulp from a glass with a slice of lemon floating in it.

'Mama,' I say hesitantly.

I want to ask her a question but I do not know how to phrase it. I want to ask why sometimes she slaps me and other times she acts like she loves me. And I want to know what I can do to make her always love me and never want to slap me anymore.

'Yes?'

'I was just wondering . . .'

'What?'

'If you like me.'

She giggles.

'Strange, strange child,' my mother says, smiling at my reflection. 'There's a juicy fruit lip gloss I bought for you in the bathroom. You can find it in the cabinet above the basin.'

I take that as a 'yes' and skip off to the bathroom.

While I'm smearing sweet-tasting grease over my lips and looking in the mirror for a gap between my own front teeth, my mother's friend Aunty Patience rushes into the bathroom unties the top of her halter-neck flared jumpsuit and peels it down past her thighs. I watch her in the mirror.

'Hey baby,' she says. 'Ooh, I am dying to pee!'

She pulls down her knickers. I glance, horrified, at the forest of black hair growing between her legs and she watches me in the mirror and laughs as I look. I am disgusted. I knew that men had tufts of wiry hair growing around their privates but I didn't know that women did too.

'Never seen a grown woman naked before?' she says, sitting on the loo, a cigarette in her hand, still laughing. 'Eddie's here. You two can hang out.'

Aunty Patience's son, Eddie is stretched out on the bed like a cat in the sun, on top of dozens of leather jackets and fur coats and colourful handbags and shawls. Eddie's skin's the colour of milky tea. His big eyes are the green of unripe strawberries. His Afro is bigger than Michael Jackson's. We've never met before but we're shut into a room together.

Mummy Elizabeth doesn't like kids running round, getting under grown-ups' feet, getting up to no good and spoiling grown-ups' parties. So she tends to shut me in the spare room, along with the coats and handbags. Even when I'm all alone, I don't mind at all. In fact, I like being told to stay in a room, where I can stand with my ear pressed against the door, eavesdropping, memorising adults' conversations, searching their handbags.

But today I am not all alone.

I'm all but ignoring the boy here with me though because I feel too shy to make eye contact. I am sitting at a gold-and-cream dressing table with my face so close to a small colour TV that I'm afraid I might end up blind. I pick up an already opened glass bottle, filled with what looks like water. There's a dead fly floating on its back inside the bottle. I know that it might contain booze and although I've never dared drink booze before, I am willing to swig it now in order to impress this Eddie whose eyes I can feel on me.

'*I'm* not afraid of no fly,' says Eddie. 'Give it here. I'll drink it.'

His voice is low-toned and he lays his words out slooow, like he doesn't give a shit whether or not you're going to agree with anything he says.

'Go on, then,' I say, offering him the bottle.

'I was only joking,' says Eddie. 'Come over here.' He pats a space next to him on the bed, on top of a cream fur coat.

We lay side by side in silence, watching telly with the volume turned off. It's this programme called *The Fosters* and I suppose there's no need for words. We just drink in the mesmerising sight of so many faces like ours, *brown* faces, on the TV.

After a bit, Eddie says, 'Do you like my jacket? It cost my dad two hundred quid.'

He's wearing a chocolate-brown jacket with a long pointed collar and is smells like real leather.

'I don't believe you,' I say.

Secretly, I *do* believe that Eddie's jacket cost two hundred quid. I am also jealous of the fact that Eddie has a dad, and a dad who buys him cool clothes, no less.

'How many times have you met your dad?'

'I see him all the time,' says Eddie. 'But my parents are divorced, aren't they? I live with my mum.'

'How come you live with your mum?'

'What do you mean?'

'How long have you lived with her?'

'Since I was a baby. My entire life. Everyone lives with their mum, don't they?'

I've never heard of a coloured kid who lived with their real mum for their entire childhood. I didn't know such a situation could exist.

'How old are you, then?' he says.

'Seven and a half,' I lie, hoping that the lip gloss my mother gave me to wear at least makes me look seven and a half.

'You look older than that,' Eddie says and I watch him looking at the way my bum sticks out behind me, as round as a football in my new too-small jeans. 'You look eight.'

He is twelve, he says.

'You know what?' says Eddie. 'You're really pretty.'

It's like being on a ferris wheel and the ride stopping suddenly, mid-air: my whole world shudders to a delicious halt the very second Eddie calls me pretty. I feel an urge to run to the nearest mirror and gaze at my myself in a new, rose-tinted light. Instead I just blush.

'Wanna see something?' he says.

I'm not sure whether I want to see what ever he's offering to show me, or not; but I can't just say no. Eddie's words have control over me now. With one spiteful word he could wipe out the glow he's planted inside me by calling me pretty, and make me feel ugly again. I'm not sure what, if anything, to do next.

'Yes or no?' he asks, yawning.

I feel the way I did when I was learning to dive and I was teetering on the edge of the swimming baths in Haslemere, watching and listening to the older kids who were treading water in the deep-end as they smirked and then chanted at me to 'Jump! Jump! Jump!'

'Ok then,' I say to Eddie. 'Show me.'

I close my eyes for a second, open them and see Eddie reach into the back of his head and pull out a silver-pronged comb that was completely hidden inside his Afro. At the very end of the comb's handle is a black hand, clenched into a fist.

'Wow!' I say.

'I'm telling you,' he says. 'This comb is righteous.'

'It is really, really cool.'

'So what's happening then, pretty?' Eddie says, sort of grinning.

I blush and shrug at the same time. I never know how to answer when the trendy kids ask, 'What's happening?'

Eddie's wearing a heavy gold ring on his middle finger with a tiny lion's head on it. His fingers – softer than I'd imagine a boy's could ever be – start dancing along the side of my face. I feel the ring, chunky and hard, rubbing against my cheek. Eddie's mouth is so close to mine that I can nearly taste the cheese and onion crisps on his breath.

'So what should we do now?' he says, resting the side of his head in the palm of his hand and breathing the question into my ear.

'Whatever you want to do. We could play cards.'

'You wanna see something else?' he says in that easy voice.

'OK then.'

Eddie flips onto his side and yawns and stretches, then smiles at me approvingly. He lays his hand on top of my hand which makes it hard to tell where my skin begins and his skin ends.

With his other hand, Eddie eases his orange corduroy flares halfway down over his hips in one long slow movement. Gently, he pushes my hand inside the waistband of his white underpants. I feel a hard, hideous-feeling wriggly lump beneath my fingers.

'That's my prick,' he says.

I know, I think. I know, I know.

There is something deeply wrong with me.

Something ugly in the way I walk, smile, smell, talk, that makes men – and now, boys – want to do certain things. Show me things. Show me their privates. And not just show me their things and then run off, the way I've heard flashers do.

The grown-up men who trail after me want to make me dirty and disgusting. They want me to feel and become so dirty that I can't tell on them, because if I did tell, no one I love would love me anymore.

When I was younger, before I started primary school, my mother had a boyfriend. Denny. He was the first one I can remember. She'd go out shopping and to the hair salon and Denny would babysit me. I'd sit there doing my colouring and he'd play Boney M records and read magazines filled with pictures of ladies.

I still see him. Denny. I see him all the time, especially at night. In my nightmares. Nanny has never understood why I wake up screaming at least once a week. And I've never told. I see Denny's teeth, which are huge. I hear his laugh, which is surprisingly soft, like a sheep bleating or something, the sort of laugh you could wrap yourself up in. He has strange tastes. He likes to slice up cucumbers length-ways and dip them in salt before eating them. He likes to sit me in his lap and lay kisses all the way up and down my arms.

He kept saying, 'You look just like a little version of your mother.'

'Feel it then,' says Eddie. 'Touch it.'

'OK then,' I say. My voice sounds like it's coming from far away, like it's not coming from my own body.

I lie on my side, staring bleakly at the bedroom door behind Eddie's head as he slowly manoeuvres my numb hand up and down and up and down the length of the thing inside his pants. I have not even a shred of willpower.

The feel of Eddie's prick inside my hand, this rhythmic movement, makes memories of being much younger, much smaller erupt from where I had buried them long ago. Denny, my mother's old boyfriend, wore these weird jeans that had buttons instead of a zip, which I found strange. When he pulled those jeans down and I saw – for the first time – the horribly wrinkly sacs hanging down against his thighs, everything started fading in and out of focus, like a flickering TV screen.

Fragments of images. A bush of wiry hair smashing against my mouth. Feeling myself choking. Hearing myself spluttering. All this happening in broad daylight right in my mother's parlour, which meant, despite how disgusting it seemed, it must be normal. Normal, like a baby drinking milk from a bottle or sucking on its dummy, maybe. Normal like Dr Gillies putting one of those little wooden sticks down my throat so he can look at my tonsils. Normal.

I remember a scream caught in my throat like a too-big particle of food. I remember gliding into a dark place where I held my breath and clenched every muscle so fiercely that even my tongue was rigid. Then the little girl they still call Anita shattered into tiny bits and the broken pieces flew into space and nothing much was left of her at all. Except numbness. And nightmares. And the ability to pretend to be OK.

Now I think to myself: I'll do whatever Eddie asks. But I won't *do* anything: I'll let him do whatever *he* wants to do. As long as I keep completely still and just lie here and do not take part in this, and do not think about what is going on, then this is not really happening to me. Not the real me, the precious and untouched part of me I keep protected inside like an unborn baby. My body's a nasty dish-rag that I can evacuate whenever I want and return to only when I absolutely have to.

'Eddie,' I say, still not daring to look up at him. 'Do you like me?'

'Yeah,' says Eddie. 'I do like you.'

But even though I try to separate myself from what is happening to me, a sneaky, traitorous part of me wants to be liked, wants to know that Eddie wants to do this because of me, not just simply because I'm there and it's something to do.

He tries to slip his other hand inside the waistband of my jeans, but the jeans are skin-tight and there's no space between denim and flesh. He moves my hand faster inside his pants. Then he gives me a smile that's like a ray of unexpected sunlight. In the dim light Eddie's green eyes seem to glitter a bit, like marbles. I know I'm not supposed to be letting him make me touch him like this but his approval of me feels good. I shut my eyes. If I don't actually see his thing it's as though this is not happening.

And then the bedroom door swings open.   ·

The little room fills with voices and music. A woman in a gold lace wrapper, with her hair done up in a huge melon style, bounces into the room. I smell her yeasty champagne -breath. Barely looking at me or Eddie, the woman snatches up a golden handbag from the floor, reaches inside it and pulls out a lighter.

Eddie winks at me. He wriggles back into his trousers and drags me through the now open door and into the group of grown-ups who are twirling and sweating in my mother's parlour. The sweet, thick, oily scent of fried plantains hangs in the stale air of the parlour, mingling with the whiff of hot armpits, hot pepper and Sta Sof Fro spray. Making me want to puke.

My favourite record is playing. Michael Jackson's thin voice sails out of my mother's speakers singing the track 'I Want You Back'. I'm glad it's dark. No one can look at me. I feel lumpy in my too-tight new clothes. And I feel I'm overflowing with filth.

Eddie lowers his eyelids as he moves to the music. He spins around, lifts one knee, sinks almost to the ground, gets up, spins around and touches the Afro comb stuck in the back of his head.

I move around on the dance floor just enough not to draw attention to myself among the dancing, swirling bodies. I stand opposite Eddie with my long arms held stiffly at my sides, concentrating hard on staying in rhythm with the music as I move one leg behind me and back to the centre and then the other leg behind me and back.

I steal glances at Eddie. I wonder if the slimy stuff that must lurk inside his willie, the disgusting stuff that I know he wanted to empty out into my hand, will instead leak out inside his orange cords; staining them. Ruining them.

Eddie stops dancing after a while, looks at me and says, 'Don't you know how to dance?'

'I *am* dancing.'

He thinks about this and then bursts out laughing 'Yeah, right,' says Eddie. 'Dream on.'

He touches the Afro comb in his head again and keeps dancing.

Humiliated, I turn away from him and look at my Aunty Adaeze who is doing a dance my mother calls the 'funky chicken' and crooning, 'Hey, hey' in time to the music. I envy Aunty Adaeze's lack of self-consciousness; her obvious joy in her own body. She curls a finger, beckoning me over to her.

'Where's my Aunty Onyi?' I ask her. I want to feel Aunty Onyi's thick brown arms around me, pressing me into her solid motherly flesh and hugging me and never letting me go.

Then my mother cuts in front of me, swaying gently to the music and carrying a silver container filled to the brim with ice cubes.

'Who let you out?' she says. And with her bony knee in the small of my back she nudges me towards a row of brand-new dining chairs whose seats are still wrapped in plastic.

'Sit down and stay down,' she says. 'And stop dancing like that. It's an embarrassment.'

I sit down, as instructed. I watch the party reach a crescendo and then wind down again before my eyes and I sit there through it all, feeling completely distanced from everybody in the room.

Racialism

WE TURN RIGHT, ONTO Woodview, passing tall red letters, spray-painted across a garage door: WOGS OUT. PAKIS DIE. NF.

And here I was, thinking I was home now, and safe. I've been longing to get home, to disappear inside Nanny's puffy white arms. And now these words, blood-coloured words. Were they written as a warning specifically to me?

There has – had – always been a sort of grudging tolerance of me on Woodview, or so I thought. No one – not even the handful of skins on the estate – has ever tried to kick my head in. The worst thing that's happened was a drunken skin accosting me when I was walking home from Brownies one night with Aunty Wendy. 'Mind yourself, nigger,' he snarled.

Aunty Wendy snarled back, 'You ought to be ashamed of yourself, picking on a little girl, you racialist bastard,' and the skinhead scuttled away without another word.

Aunty Adaeze glances out of the car window, at the same blood-red words I'm seeing. But she doesn't comment.

'Nice weather today, eh?' she says. 'It's cooled down a bit.'

Pulling up outside number 52, Mummy Elizabeth toots her horn again and again until Nanny appears in the doorway of our house, holding a piece of kitchen towel. My mother lowers the car window.

'Is Agnes inside?'

'No, Lizzy,' says Nanny. 'I think she's at work.'

'She doesn't work on Sundays, Nanny,' I say. 'Remember? She's probably round Aunty Wendy's.'

Nanny grimaces at my comment. Then she says, 'By the way, Lizzy,' and a cheeky, crooked little smile appears on her face making the wrinkles at the corners of her mouth deepen. 'Mrs Tucker next door's found someone to take in Judy. There's nothing for you to worry about at all, Lizzy. The little dog's gone.'

Judy. Gone? The grown-ups' behaviour is confusing me to the point where it's making my head hurt. If Judy has really gone, why on earth's Nanny grinning like the Cheshire Cat?

My mother, Aunty Adaeze and I continue on to 16 Acacia Way: Aunty Wendy and Uncle Mick's house.

'Anita,' Mummy Elizabeth says, without even turning around to look at me. 'I've got a feeling that Agnes is up to no good. She's never around when I look for her. What is she up to?'

I shrug my bare shoulders and look out the window. I've no idea why Agnes makes a point of being out when my mother visits. One of the Scott brothers across the road sees me and sticks two fingers up at me. I mouth the words 'You can get lost' and clench my fist at him through the car window, thinking of the black fist on Eddie's Afro comb.

My mother slides out of the driver's seat and walks up the front path and raps on Aunty Wendy's front door. She balances on one toe of her Italian shoes – fawn with gold detailing today – and then on the other, waiting for Aunty Wendy to come to the door.

'Hello, love,' she says when she finally opens the door. 'Hello, Lizzy. Hello, Ada. Did you have a lovely time in London, Neet?'

'No,' I almost say. But then, instinctively, I nod.

'We are looking for Agnes,' my mother says.

'Oh yes,' says Aunty Wendy, standing there in her blue triangle-shaped skirt. 'I think Aggy'd like you to meet her friend, Barry. He's a lovely lad, isn't he, Neet?'

'Don't know,' I say.

'Aggy and Barry have just gone up the shop. They'll be back in a minute, Lizzy.'

In the sitting room my mother, Aunty Adaeze and I occupy the whole sofa. Suddenly, Aunty Adaeze and my mother scream in unison as Judy appears from nowhere and tries to rub her shaggy little head against my mother's legs. I am so happy and relieved that I feel almost like kissing my mother.

'What is this little witch?' screams Aunty Adaeze, inching away from Judy who is threatening to jump onto the sofa and into Aunty Adaeze's lap.

'This is the final straw!' my mother hisses, hopping up from the sofa.

And then we all see it, at the same time. Agnes sliding along the hall, holding hands with a tall, long-legged white boy who is thin, like a rasher of bacon. It's her boyfriend, Barry, and he whispers something that makes Agnes tip her head back and chuckle. Agnes's face is shining with happiness – until she sees Mummy Elizabeth and Aunty Adaeze through the open sitting-room door. She peers furtively at us, looks up at Barry and whispers,

'*Kedu*, Aunty Adaeze? Mum? This is my . . . umm . . . friend, Barry.'

'He's ever such a nice boy, Lizzy,' Aunty Wendy claims again.

My mother's face writhes with outrage.

'A *white* boy,' she whispers. She sits, unmoving, her lower lip wobbling as if she's about to cry. 'A *white* boy?'

Aunty Adaeze covers my mother's delicate hand with her own man-like one.

'OK, Elizabeth,' she says her orange and gold wrapper crackling. 'I will handle this.'

'No,' says Mummy Elizabeth. 'No.' And with that, my mother runs into the kitchen and begins throwing open the drawers beneath the sink. I see something flash in her hand. She raises it high above her head: Aunty Wendy's new carving knife that gleams in the late afternoon sun spilling through the kitchen window.

Barry spins on his heel and legs it out of the back door. My mother goes after him but her dress gets caught on a corner of the rabbit hutch in the garden. Barry doesn't stop to look at the sight of Mummy Elizabeth on her back with one bare toe poking through the grid of the rabbits' cage. With his long legs he sails right over the top of the garden gate and out of sight. And, just as quickly, my mother picks herself up, grabs the fallen carving knife, hitches up her dress and leaps clean over the closed garden gate, yelling, 'Come back here, you lout!'

Aunty Adaeze, Agnes, Judy, Aunty Wendy, two of the neighbours and I hover outside the garden gate, in the square. I am trembling so much that my teeth are chattering.

'You all right, Neet?' says one of our neighbours, who's standing with her hands on her huge hips, relishing the unexpected drama. 'You look cold, love.'

I am in a trance. I say nothing.

Still carrying the carving knife, my mother comes stalking back towards us. 'He x-scaped,' she hisses, dropping the knife on the floor.

She glares at Agnes and then grabs Aunty Adaeze's hand and the two of them flounce through the hall out the front door and into the car.

'Our mother is a flipping mental racist cow,' says Agnes. 'And there's nothing that woman can do that will stop me from loving Barry.'

Agnes doesn't look much like Agnes any more. For the first time in my life, her hair looks quite a bit worse than mine. She's wearing one of Nanny's blue nylon shirtwaister dresses and the dress hangs limply from her shoulders like a huge blue potato sack.

This hideous change in Agnes's appearance is my mother's

doing. After chasing Barry out of Aunty Wendy's, my mother and Aunty Adaeze had burst into Nanny's house, stormed up the stairs into Agnes's box room and tossed everything they found there into bin bags. When Nanny asked them what on earth they thought they were doing, she was warned 'Stay out of this.' Finally, with the bin bags on the back seat of the car, they'd driven back to London.

The good thing about my mother's 'outburst', as Nanny calls it, is that now Agnes talks to me more than she ever has before. She spends hours every day telling me how much she loves Barry and how much she hates our mother.

'*That cow* only acted like that because Barry's white, innit?' she says.

'So they'd like him if he was coloured, then?'

'Yeah. Or at least they wouldn't try to knife him.'

'But what about if he was half-caste?'

'They'd cut him in half and only keep the black part.'

Agnes and I look at each other and burst out laughing.

'What would you have done if she killed him?' I say.

'What?'

'What if our mother or Adaeze had killed him?'

'It's *Aunty* Adaeze.'

'All right,' I say. I poke my tongue out at Agnes.

'You need to learn respect,' she says, looking very cross. 'You don't have no respect for anything. And it's your fault, anyway. You're the one who told them I was at Wendy's.'

'It's *Aunty* Wendy.'

'Oh my God. I am so sick of you!' she says.

I hop off the bed and walk to Agnes's tiny bedroom window, turning my back on her. Aggy glides up behind me and presses her palms down on my shoulders.

'What's wrong,' she says. 'Are you crying? Come here. I'm not really sick of you.'

I stand on tiptoes to pull apart the curtains and gaze out at the

69

nearly black sky, looking for stars. I'm not sure why I am crying. All I know is that I feel clogged up with secrets, with filth. That I have absolutely nobody in my life I trust enough to tell.

'Come on, what's wrong?' Agnes says, trying to turn me around so that I'll face her. 'I *know* you, Anita. You haven't been the same since you came back from London. You've been walking around saying nothing, like a ghost.'

I want to tell her what happened in London. But I can't. I want to tell her how I feel like I'm sliding down into someplace that's dark like the inside of a coffin, some place I can never, ever be rescued from. The right words don't come. I can't find them.

'It's just that I'm worried about my spelling test tomorrow,' I say finally.

'Anita, why? You'll probably come top, just like you win everything,' says Agnes. 'I wish I could come top in something.'

I feel a wall sliding between Agnes and me, with Agnes on one side, and on the other side the girl Agnes thinks I am. And in between, squashed against the wall, is the real me.

Going Home

'THIS IS WHAT I gave up, Nin,' says Nanny, pressing a miniature pork pie into her mouth. 'I gave up all of this, for love.'

We are parked near a driveway on the outskirts of Selsey.
Sitting in Nanny's car, munching our way through a packet of
little gourmet Marks and Sparks pies. Drinking in the sight
of the tallest, widest mansion I have ever seen. The mansion
is painted white and it has a pointed grey roof. Green triangle-shaped trees are dotted in front of the house, as though
guarding it.

'Nip out of the car and round the side there and see if you can
see anything through the windows,' says Nanny. 'I'd give anything
to know who lives in there now.'

Nanny always seems to be asking me to spy on people (mainly
on Agnes or my mother) and then report back on what I've seen
and learned. Like I'm a walking, talking, tabloid newspaper. It's
not that I dislike spying – I'm a masterful eavesdropper – it's just
that I mind being ordered around.

But of course I have to do as I am told. I trot across the
driveway and the loud crunch of the gravel beneath my plimsolls makes me fear the owner will hear me and demand to
know what a wild-haired coloured girl is doing darting up his
drive.

I smooth down my hair, which for days has not been combed
properly, and it springs right back up. I stand on tiptoes, balancing against the side of the house. I crane my neck and try to peer

into the lowest of the windows, but the windows are covered by white wooden shutters. I can't see a thing.

Before her dad lost all his money at the horse races, before she married Gramps, Nanny used to live inside this same gigantic house, with her parents.

Her dad was an engineer, I think, and Nanny and her parents and her younger brother Frank had riding lessons, tennis courts, horses, *money*. Her parents had their own housekeeper. Then she met Gramps, who was poor but kind and who had a movie-star smile. Nanny forgot all about money and from that day onwards she never really had any.

'It wasn't easy after I got married,' Nanny says, staring at the house as she eats another little pie. 'My dad was a Jew, so he always had a lot of money. At first my father gave me an allowance but that was humiliating for Matt. He said he wanted to be able to support his own wife. But he had no money. Do you remember Great-Grandpa, darling?'

Great-Grandpa was Nanny's dad and he died when I was very small. I remember a thin man with a long thick nose.

'Didn't Gramps have any money?' I say.

'No, Nin, darling. He came from a poor family. His mum was just a young girl, a servant, and we think the man she worked for had his way with her. Matt never did know who his father was. There was nothing more humiliating – then – than growing up knowing you were illegitimate. He never got over it.'

'What does it mean, Nanny? Illegitimate?'

'It means that your mother and father aren't married.'

'Am I illegitimate?'

Nanny doesn't answer.

'Are we poor now, Nanny?'

I'm pretty sure we are. We don't get those little brown envelopes fat with fivers and tenners that the other families get every Friday.

'Money doesn't really matter when you've got love, darling.'

*   *   *

The time of having odd days off school, going for long drives and then sitting watching things began after Gramps died. There was a funeral for Gramps; my mother and Agnes went to it, but I wasn't allowed to go – Nanny said I was too young. Instead Nanny and I said our private farewell to Gramps a little while after the funeral. The two of us drove to Lily Pond, one of Nanny's favourite spots, and spent an hour gazing at a heron. I demolished two packs of salt and vinegar crisps. I tried not to cry, and failed.

Since losing the love of her life, Nanny's changed. It's like I've become almost a grown-up in her eyes. All of a sudden I get away with a lot. Aunty Wendy says my behaviour's getting ridiculous and Aggy says my spoiled bitchness is 'becoming a joke'. But no one can put their finger on precisely what's wrong with my behaviour – all they know is it's getting irritating. Nanny's far too indulgent, everyone says.

If Nanny catches me with my light on, still reading when it's close to midnight, she just says, 'You still awake then? You'll be ever so tired in the morning if you don't go to sleep soon, Nin.' And leaves me be.

One night, having read all of the books in my bedroom at least twice, I wander downstairs. Nanny is asleep upright in her blue armchair. The phone receiver, wrapped in a piece of kitchen towel, is resting in her lap.

I slip into the kitchen, open the cupboard, take a Wagon Wheel and slide the whole biscuit into my mouth. I linger by the sink, feeling like a well-fed cobra and I just can't take my naughty little eyes off the taps. I reach up and turn on the cold water. I long to know *why* Nanny won't touch the taps without a piece of kitchen towel being present to protect her skin. Would her skin melt if the tap touched her?

I rub my hand against the cold tap again and again. Nothing happens. Any minute now I am sure to hear Nanny's voice hissing, *What the hell are you doing touching things in my kitchen, you dirty little bitchie?* Or Aggy might spring down the stairs and call me a weirdo. But my curiosity won't let me stop.

I run my hand along the back-door handle. I slowly turn it and it makes a sound like the grating laughter of an ancient man, making me leap back. Then I skim my fingers over the rubbish bin lid and smear them across the fridge door. Nothing happens.

I tiptoe across the room and peer round the sitting-room door to check Nanny's still asleep.

But her eyes are wide open. Tears are oozing out of them.

I rush to her side and pat her arm. I often find her crying to herself nowadays – I think she's crying because she still misses Gramps.

'Don't worry, I wasn't doing anything, Nanny,' I say, feeling very mature.

'What are you on about, Nin?' Her voice is cracking, her eyes averted.

'Your mother,' she says finally. 'She rang up just now and told me, Nin. Darling, she's gone and bought you a ticket to Africa. You'll be there before Christmas.'

'*Africa?* Will I ever come back?'

'I don't know, Anita. I don't know.'

'But she'll probably forget to come and get me anyway and go to Africa by herself, without me. Won't she?'

'I doubt it. Who could afford to waste the kind of money she must have spent on your aeroplane ticket? Must have cost her five hundred pounds for a journey like that.'

An icy little thrill runs through me at the thought of somebody spending five hundred pounds on me. And then, just like that, the thrill is gone.

'But I don't want to go,' I say, my voice quivering.

I absolutely do not want to be alone with the maniac who calls herself my mother. Ever since she tried to slash up Agnes's boyfriend, Barry, I've had this feeling that my mother, or one of her sisters, might just knife me next time I annoy her.

'I know, darling. I know,' says Nanny. 'It breaks my heart to even have to think of letting you go. I feel so helpless . . .'

Nanny's voice disintegrates into an inaudible whisper. She begins weeping again and I sit on the edge of her armchair, holding her hand. I feel an unnatural, dazed sense of calm. I sit holding Nanny's hand, wondering – in a detached, disinterested way – what piece of my life is about to be ripped off my back next.

Early the next morning, Nanny rings up Mr Clifford, my headmaster. She tells him in a shrill, on-the-verge-of-tears voice that I'll be missing the last week of term because I'm going to Africa for who knows how long.

Mrs Pope, the art teacher with the free-flowing greying blond hair, the flapping corduroy flares and the cheesecloth smocks, just cannot keep my grim news to herself. 'One lucky little girl here is going somewhere very special and exciting for Christmas this year,' she announces to the class.

Sitting cross-legged on the classroom floor, everyone turns their heads to spot the kid she's talking about and I keep a neutral expression on my face, hoping nobody will guess. If only Mrs Pope would shut up . . . But Mrs Pope is thrilled. Not because she wants to get rid of me and lose me to Africa but rather because she thinks my 'links' to Africa are a wonderful thing. She's said, before now, that I'm exotic. She's told me I need to get into expressing my 'roots' in my artwork.

'Anita is going to Nigeria in Africa for the holidays!' Mrs Pope exclaims, grinning like crazy. 'Can anyone point out Nigeria on the map?'

Why can't the grey classroom floor be made of quicksand so that I can be swallowed up? Why can't God stop Mrs Pope from unwittingly reminding all my classmates that I should be holding a spear, not a paintbrush.

'Does anyone know where Nigeria is on the map?' asks Mrs Pope again.

You'll never catch me sticking my hand up and drawing attention to myself. When I was five I once wet my knickers in class rather than ask for permission to go to the loo. My school reports say, 'Excellent potential but needs to participate more in class.' Sometimes I am so ready to speak up that I can *taste* the answer on my tongue. But I stay quiet. I'm afraid that my truth is not the accepted truth.

'Anita, do you know the answer to this question?' a teacher will ask. 'You look like you're bursting to say something.'

I'll shake my head.

'Can nobody show me where Nigeria is on the map?'

Someone pipes up, 'No, Miss.'

The rest of us shake our heads. We either don't know or don't care to say where Nigeria is on the map.

'Nigeria must be where all the nig-nogs come from,' whispers Andrew and I feel too embarrassed to turn around and glare at him.

At the end of our lesson, Mrs Pope asks me to stay behind. I sit there watching her wipe off the blackboard. I adore our classroom when it's empty. There is silence, apart from the sound of our class hamster creeping through the shredded paper in its cage.

'Why the long face?' she says. 'Africa will be wonderful, fabulous – especially at Christmas – how exciting! And Nigeria! They have incredible rainforests there.'

The next day in Art, I take a huge piece of paper and begin to paint. To me, paint-brushes are magic wands and I love letting my hand meander. I paint a forest of trees, like the ones in the woods in Fernmere but with pineapples hanging off them instead of green leaves. I paint myself standing underneath one of the pineapple trees, crying my eyes out, with my little navy suitcase at my feet. Four trees behind me is a fat orange tiger, waiting to pounce, its red tongue hanging out from its sharp-toothed mouth. At the bottom of the picture, in wide pink letters, I scrawl 'Miss Biafra in the Rainforest'.

Mrs Pope pins my painting up on the wall. Every day, I look up at it and think of hideous Africa. I look at my picture so many times that I can taste the sweetness of those pineapples and feel the sharpness of the tiger's teeth and nails. It's the opposite of an Advent Calendar: a daily reminder that I'll soon be facing the worst day of my life: the day I leave for Africa.

Agnes is the only one of us who likes the thought of going to Africa. The excitement mounts in her as the dread grows in me. But ironically Agnes may not be able to go to Africa: my mother's refusing to buy her a ticket until she promises never to see unsuitable Barry ever again.

Two weeks before I'm due to leave for Nigeria, Nanny and I kneel side by side on the floor at the foot of my frilly pink bed. My bedside lamp is on and I can see little beige cake crumbs caught in the grey whiskers that grow from the corner of Nanny's mouth. I'm worried that if I open my mouth to say a prayer out loud, one of the dangling cake crumbs will drop into my mouth.

'Who do we ask when we want something badly?' says Nanny, the crumbs moving as she speaks. 'We ask Gentle Jesus. We have to pray, Nin. Let's pray that your mother doesn't turn up and that you won't have to go to Africa.'

I don't see the point in saying prayers out loud; if Jesus really is the son of God, I'd have thought he could simply read our minds. I bet Jesus already knows about the things I pray for silently: to live in the United States of America with my dad, to have my own typewriter and to become so pretty that strangers grow jealous and people who know me whisper, 'Bugger me that Anita's grown into a pretty girl.' I pray to become one of those clean, prized girls. Like a private-school white girl. Never touched against my will, never even laughed at.

And I silently beg Gentle Jesus to send my father to the rescue.

I close my eyes and bow my head and an image of my father floats into my mind. My father will look very much like Huggy Bear, the coloured man in *Starsky & Hutch*. My father will have a helicopter, which will be filled with Puffin paperbacks. (The one detail my mother's shared about my father is that he loves to read and was always surrounded by books when she knew him). Before my mother can whisk me off to Africa, my father will open his helicopter door, take off his sunglasses and reach out his hand to me.

'Precious,' he will say, because I'm sure my father was the person who named me Precious. 'Hop in, I want you to come and live in the United States with me.'

I will take one long last look at my mother, who'll be standing there shaking her head and saying, 'There's nothing *I* can do to stop him. He's your father.'

On the day I am to leave for Africa, Nanny and I sit staring nervously at my suitcases for two hours, waiting for my mother to show. Finally, the phone rings. My mother instructs Nanny to drive me to Haslemere train station and put me on a train that will deliver me to her.

My mother no longer lives in her flat; she has moved to a large house on a never-ending street where spindly, swaying trees teeter close to the kerbs. She lets me sit on the wall outside her new house while she slips inside to finish packing. I steal glances at an older girl who is sitting on the wall in front of the house next door.

'I'm Cynthia. Who are you?' the girl says.

'My mum lives here,' I whisper.

'I've never seen you before in my life.'

Her black hair is shiny and flat, hanging down her back like a white girl's.

'How did you get your hair like that?'

'At the hair salon,' Cynthia says, tossing her head so that her hair bounces against her back. 'I have it relaxed.'

She looks at me very carefully, from toe to head, as though deciding whether to share a secret with me or not.

'There's something in your back garden,' she says.

'What?'

'Go into your back garden. I'll follow.'

She disappears into her house and I disappear into my mother's house. When I reach the back, Cynthia is climbing over a wire fence into my mother's garden. She picks up a stick and points to what appears to be a torn piece of fur coat. As we get really close to the furry mass, a sickly almost sweet smell seeps up into our nostrils. It's a dead rat with dried blood on its mouth and flies wandering over its body.

'How did it die?' I say.

'Who cares?' says Cynthia. 'I don't know.'

She pokes the rat with her stick. I nudge it with my foot.

I am desperate to impress this cool-looking girl. I haven't had a coloured friend since Effua left and I would love to make friends with Cynthia. But my innate inquisitiveness (or as Agnes calls it, 'natural weirdness') takes over. I crouch down and with the very tip of my finger, I touch the dead rat's fur.

Cynthia screams.

'You are fucking crazy,' she says, stepping back. 'You've probably got fleas now.'

She eyes me suspiciously.

'Why does your mum live in there all by herself and we've never seen her with any daughter? Where have you been living all this time?'

'With my nanny. And it's not just me; I've got a sister too.'

'Have not!'

'Ask my mum!'

'I doubt she'd speak to me. Africans are stuck-up, they hate people like me. I'm Jamaican.'

'Oh,' I say, afraid now to tell her that I'm on my way to Africa.

*   *   *

Inside my mother's new house there's no Christmas tree. I make a mental note of this. It is a detail that I will remember to delight Nanny and Aunty Wendy. I silently rehearse what I'll say: 'She's so mean that she doesn't even have a Christmas tree in her house. Can you imagine that?'

My mother does not have a Christmas tree but her parlour floor is decorated with bags: Harrods carrier bags, open leather suitcases. I tiptoe around and over them. In the middle of the expensive chaos, my mother is crouching like a frog, balancing on her cashmere-soft bare feet and humming some kind of tune in a high-pitched tone. A gold bracelet that's so thin it looks like it could cut into the skin adorns her delicate wrist.

The carpet in this new parlour feels like the coat of an unshorn sheep. I sink my knees deep into the pile and watch my mother folding clothes up and fishing more clothes out of carrier bags and unwrapping them, laying them out on the floor and stroking them. She stops humming and slides her eyes towards my face.

'What?' she says.

'Nothing.'

'I can see that you're itching to ask me something. I can tell.'

'Is it weird that I don't live with you?'

'Oh no! Not *this* rubbish again.'

I try again. 'Do you like having me as your daughter?'

'What the hell are you talking about now? Of course I like having you. You're my daughter.'

'Why don't I ever see my dad? I want to see him.' My voice is so soft I can barely hear myself speak.

'You think that man really has any interest in you?'

I am not going to let my mother bulldoze away my sense of hope in my dad. I raise my chin and look defiantly into her fierce eyes.

'Yes, I *know* he has an interest in me.'

She drops a pink sweater onto the floor, raises her hand as if to slap me but then flexes her wrist so that her palm forms a stop sign in front of my face.

'It hasn't been easy for me,' she says, shaking her head.

'What do you mean, Mum?'

'Nothing.' She turns her head a little to the right, as though somebody is about to snap a photo of her. She tilts her nose towards the ceiling and then sweeps her eyes down to my level. 'Whatever you think, I *love* you, Nitty.'

It is the first time I can remember my mother saying 'I love you' out loud to me, although she has written the words down before, in birthday cards.

'Thank you, Mummy. I love you too.'

I shuffle over to her on my knees and hug her around the waist. Her bones feel fragile and light. She wriggles out of my embrace like an impatient schoolgirl. I watch her as she grabs a pair of white sandals, still joined together by a price tag, and holds them up in front of my face.

'Look at these!' she says, flinging the sandals into my lap. 'Italian leather! This,' she says, holding up a pink sundress with shining ribbons for sleeves, 'is from Harrods. These are the new clothes I bought for you; to wear in Nigeria.'

Quicker than I can grab hold of them, my mother tosses more brand-new clothes in my direction and I try to catch them.

'And this,' she squeals. 'And this! Look at this! Look at! Look at!'

There is a sea of white and pink and powder-blue clothes and shoes at my feet.

'Can't you see, Nitty? Why would I even be bothered with all this if I didn't love you so much?'

I nod, and finally, finally, I begin to understand my mother.

Here is her love for me: these clothes, still wrapped in cellophane, landing at my feet. I'm my mother's child and in her mind a child is not an individual; a child is a possession. Loving me, for her, means making me look glossy and expensive. I am a doll that can be dressed up and shown off back home. Proof my mother's has made it in the United Kingdom. Although it turns out that I'm a very odd and annoying kind of doll because I talk and constantly ask questions.

'Mummy. Can I ask you a question please?'

'Go ahead, Nitty.'

'Do you think one day you might be able to buy me a salamander costume?'

'A what?'

'It's a type of lizard, Mummy. My friend Julia's mum bought her one.'

'Your white friend's mother is buying her child *lizards*?'

'No, Mummy. A lizard *costume*. If you get it for me I could wear it on Christmas Day in Africa!'

'You want to walk around dressed like a lizard?'

I nod gently.

'Why?'

'Uncle Mick said I'd look smart in it.'

'It worries me, Nitty. The type of nonsense they are planting into your mind in Fernmere.'

My mother picks up a pair of pink-and-cream striped dungarees and tosses them into a suitcase. 'When I was younger, when I still had money, I used to buy all of your clothes in Italy. Nobody, *nobody* can ever tell me that my daughter is not imm-ac-u-lately dressed. But I get sick of all your questions. I'm the one who's paid for you all these years and you're not even one bit grateful, are you?'

'I'm sorry, Mummy. I *am* grateful. I *do* understand.'

On the top of my C&A bag that Aunty Wendy, Uncle Mick and Nanny have stuffed with wrapped Christmas gifts, there is a second-hand Sindy doll that Uncle Mick handed me earlier in the day, as a going-away present. I fish Sindy out and lay her on top of all my new clothes, in the beige suitcase. My mother lowers the lid of the suitcase and tells me to kneel on it while she tries to do it up.

*   *   *

I am so excited and nervous about being on an aeroplane that, for the moment, my sadness at leaving Nanny and Aunty Wendy and Uncle Mick recedes. A smiling crème-caramel-coloured air hostess hands me a little tray with my tea on it. My mother looks at the air hostess and makes a sort of hissing sound by sucking at her teeth. 'That girl is nowhere near as beautiful as I looked when I was an air hostess for Air Nigeria,' she says.

The air hostess seems to overhear her and with a wooden smile she asks her if she'd like another glass of wine and my mother says, 'Yes, give me white wine.'

I examine my food. The strips of a stringy meat that tastes the way I'm sure cardboard would taste; mushy green vegetables covered in a sticky brown gravy and a very small cube of yellow cake. I cut into a strip of meat and accidentally elbow my mother while I am doing so.

'Is this lion meat?' I ask her.

'For God's sake, Anita,' my mother says. 'What's up with you?'

Even *I* am embarrassed by all the very silly questions that I am asking today, but I can't help it. Sitting next to my mother is like being a contestant on a TV gameshow. You only get a limited amount of time to answer questions and win a prize; the prize in my case being answers.

I take this opportunity to find out more about my mother's new neighbour Cynthia by asking what Jamaicans are.

'Now, why are you asking me about Jamaicans?'

'I just heard of them and wondered what they were. That's all.'

'Jamaicans,' my mother spits out the word, as if she's saying 'bitch' or 'bastard', 'are terrible, low-class people; they're stupid and lazy and uneducated. Hardly any of them even have jobs.'

She sips her wine and her eyes gleam with something that looks like mischief.

'Jamaicans are a disgrace,' she continues. 'Let me tell you, Anita; there are some real idiots in this world and not only the Jamaicans, either. Those rubbish people in Fernmere that you love so much are just as bad! They haven't travelled! They haven't been educated! Those people don't even own passports. But I will tell you one thing: whatever you hear me say about old Nanny, nobody can deny that she can talk properly. Nanny's voice sounds just like the Queen's. That's why I chose her to mind you and listen now to how you speak just like her!' My mother sinks back in her seat. 'If you were talking on the phone and the person at the other end couldn't see you, they would think you were white. I cannot even tell you how many doors that opens for you.'

My mother sips more wine and begins to fall asleep. I turn around and look for Aggy. She's sitting several rows behind us because her ticket wasn't bought until much later, after she'd finally convinced my mother that Barry was out of her life for good. Agnes waves at me and mouths: 'You all right?'

I shrug my shoulders at her.

The aeroplane is packed with noisy grown-ups squeezed into small seats and they are constantly opening and shutting the plastic things that cover the windows and clicking their fingers to try and get the pretty air hostesses' attention. Aggy seems very small and well behaved sitting among them in her white cardigan. She also looks very happy and at peace, which makes me jealous because I'm scared. I've no idea what's waiting for me when I get off this aeroplane.

Everything Is Everything

I STRUGGLE OUT OF my pink anorak and feel a huge puff of heat wrapping itself, hot and clinging and wet, around my face and body. Agnes takes a very long, very loud deep breath and says, 'Home!' and I imagine the red-hot steam she must have just sucked up into her big nostrils.

This scary, suffocating heat is not the biggest surprise about Africa. The thing that shocks me most is the people, and how much clothing they wear. There are giggling, chattering women in floor-length dresses with huge bundles of colourful material swirled around their sweating heads and big bright sashes looped around their waists. Men are walking around wearing both trousers and what look like dresses at the same time. There is no nakedness here. Not a sign of the bare boobs I have seen in Gramps's pictures. Not a single one of the distended brown bellies I've seen in programmes about Africa on TV.

I hear Uncle Mick's voice in my head. 'The people over there don't wear no clothes, do they? Bet they'll bloody well make you run around in the nude too,' he teased me before I set off.

I want to ring up Uncle Mick and tell him that so far I've seen no lions and no tigers, no cannibals, no simmering cauldrons of cooking human flesh, not even one spear-throwing native or a single monkey. If I could ring him up, I doubt Uncle Mick would even believe me. He'd say, 'You must still be in London then, musn't you? Not in Africa.'

I'm not sure whether it's from relief or the heat, but I stand there giggling to myself like some kind of lunatic and I find that I can't stop giggling, not even when my mother pinches me on the arm and says 'Shut up.'

As I watch, a woman with skin the shade and texture of sandpaper and a very fat, bulging neck sobs then falls into the arms of a tall thin rust-coloured man who hugs her quickly and walks away, into the airport. All around, there are men and women and children whose skin is as brown as, or browner than, mine. The white people who fill the pavements everywhere else I've ever been have vanished, or become invisible. I too have become invisible because not one person stares at me or points at me or appears to notice me. No one looks at me at all, apart from the driver who has been sent to pick us up; he looks at me, looks at the little 1940s beige suitcase I'm carrying, reaches out his wrinkled hand and says, 'Let me take.'

Our driver, who has no more than five teeth in his mouth, tosses our suitcases into the boot of his brown car as though they weighed no more than balls of cotton wool. I watch the driver's liquorice-black hand turning the tattered steering wheel and wonder at the huge knobbly bones on his wrists. The driver's neck jerks back and forward like a turkey's as he concentrates on driving us along the dusty orange roads that lead to Chukaro, the town where my mother's mother lives.

The plate slid in front of me is piled high with steaming-hot rice. On top of the rice are a couple of spoonfuls of a thick oily stew I know will be peppery-hot enough to burn the skin off the roof of my mouth. I watch my mother's mother watching me as I pick at the reddish-orange stew with the very tip of my fork. She claps her hands twice and says something very quickly, making clicking sounds as she speaks.

'Your grandmother said that when she last saw you as a baby you were fat and as light in complexion as the inside of a banana,' says Aunty Onyi, whose mouth is full of un-chewed rice. 'You looked half-caste then. You were so nice and fat. My mama says you're still a fine yellow girl, but you need to eat more.'

I look down at my long, increasingly thin, brown legs and feel disappointment hit me in waves. What went so horribly wrong, and why? Why can't I become beige and beautiful and loveable like a half-caste once again?

Aunty Onyi rubs the small cluster of red bumps on my arm. 'They love biting you,' she says.

My grandmother reaches across the table, pinches my cheek hard with her soft fingers then laughs and says something else, again in this fast language that I can't understand. My eyes plead with Aunty Onyi, Aunty Nneka and Agnes for an interpretation.

'Your grandmother just said she can see her own face in your face,' says Agnes. 'But honestly, Anita, I look much more like her than you do.'

I screw my nose up at Agnes.

'Where's our mother?' I ask. 'She didn't come to breakfast. I haven't seen her all day.'

I only ask because I think it's polite for a little girl to ask after her mother. It's the way Nanny'd expect me to behave. The question is unlikely to yield an answer. People rarely know precisely where Mummy Elizabeth is. You can shut your eyes and open them again and she has gone.

'Your mama and Adaeze went to Aro-Eze,' says Aunty Nneka.

'What's that?' I say, in awe of any person able to keep tabs on my mother.

'It's the town your great-grandfather's from; where the big pink house that he built is,' says Aunty Onyi. 'Your mother went to check on the place and pay some men to do some more work on it.'

'That place is really something, it's beautiful,' says Agnes, clapping her hands for no reason that I can see. 'It's a palace, I'm telling you. It's painted pink, and it's made of real bricks.'

'Aren't all houses made of real bricks?' I say.

But I already know that all houses are not made of real bricks; my grandmother's house, the house I am living in, is made of what looks like wood and has a crooked corrugated-iron roof. From the outside, the house looks to me a little like a rubbish heap and on the inside, there's no bathroom or toilet and the water we have to wash with outside is light brown. My family's fortunes plummetted during the Biafran War and never recovered.

But still, everyone in my family here (so I am told) is *ogaranya*, which means rich. This richness is the reason we have a collection of sulky-looking ladies and girls and men waiting around to plait our hair, wash our clothes, deal with the contents of our outside toilet and do anything else we might tell them to do. These servants are the *mbi*, the poor people, and their whole families – even kids younger than me – have to spend day-in, day-out making life easier for lazy people like us. None of this seems fair to me, but Agnes says that it is fairer than her and me having to wash clothes and sweep floors ourselves.

I watch as a tiny brown lizard scuttles up the wall, its head moving in the opposite direction from its tail. I run over to the other side of the room after the lizard darts away from me and creeps onto the ceiling. I wonder if it's a salamander.

My grandmother watches and giggles. My grandmother's eyes crinkle up when she laughs, reminding me of Nanny. I wish I could ring up Nanny and laugh with her about the real live lizards and about having servants and about having to traipse outside to go to wee. But as far as I've seen, there is no phone here.

'Oh, girls, girls, darling girls,' says Aunty Onyi. 'In a few days, by Christmas Eve at the latest, dozens more of the family are coming home for the holidays. We are all going to have so much fun with each other!'

The thing about Aunty Onyi is that she is *always* saying, 'We are going to have so much fun!' I can imagine her saying it even if we were all in the middle of a car crash.

'Soon, we will all travel to Aro-Eze together to join Adaeze and your mother. So Anita can see the palace and see where she really comes from, eh?' says Aunty Onyi. 'Maybe we will even go there tomorrow.'

Everything is 'maybe' or 'soon' or 'we might'. Daily life flows easily and feels uncomplicated. Languid. Every day it turns out to be far too hot and sticky to put much effort into doing anything at all. Mostly, we sit around the plastic dining table that my mother bought my grandmother as a present, drinking orange Fanta, talking, laughing, eating and making plans to do things that we never quite get around to doing.

'Can I go outside and play, Aunty Onyi?'

'It's really still too hot, my little Precious. Aren't you going to finish eating?' says Aunty Onyi.

A girl with a head as round as a sponge cake and eyes the colour of treacle slides her face around the open door and peers into the parlour.

'Precious-Yes!' Aunty Onyi screams, fanning herself. 'Come in, come in here and see us.'

In strolls Precious-Yes, my best friend here in Chukaro.

As well as being my new best friend, Precious-Yes is one of the dozens of cousins I never even knew I had before I came here. My family, it turns out, is so big and the members of it are so keen to spend time with me, my mother and Agnes, that there is not enough space or time for me ever to be alone.

I am not even allowed to sleep by myself: I sleep under a musty and greasy mosquito net, pressed between Agnes and my snoring grandmother. My mother sleeps elsewhere in the house, with one or two of her sisters for company.

I spend my nights half-awake, dodging two sets of sharp elbows as Aggy and my grandmother roll around in their sleep. During the day, aunties, uncles and cousins I've never even heard of jostle into my grandmother's parlour. There's no stopping them because they all live on my grandmother's compound, where the houses are not joined together the way our houses are on Woodview but rather are scattered in clusters, like stars in the sky. In one of these rickety old houses lives Precious-Yes.

Precious-Yes's parents met me when I came to Africa before; when I was three years old and I'd already earned the nickname Precious-No for clinging to my mother and crying NO, NO, NO whenever anyone else tried to touch me. Precious-Yes's parents took a great liking to me (so I'm told) purely because I had been born a British Citizen; they hoped some of my 'natural good luck' would rub off onto their own newborn daughter if they named her after me.

Now Precious-Yes slides her big bottom onto a wicker seat next to me and, noticing that I'm not eating my rice and stew, she picks up my fork and begins gobbling up my food. She lowers her head so close to my plate that her flat face is almost resting on top of the rice. Precious-Yes's hair is cornrowed in a style that makes her bowed head look like a game of noughts and crosses. She has a red ribbon tied to one of her plaits.

'Precious-No,' she says, munching. 'If you go to Great Britain again, I beg, can I come and live over there with you? Tell me everything that has ever happened in Great Britain! What kinds of food do they serve you over there?'

Were I a braver girl, I'd speak up and say: I like the food there better than the food they're serving us here.

The food that's dished up here in Africa terrifies and confuses me. Everything I am given seems to be either slimy or peppery or slimy *and* peppery. Every day at around noon, the house-girl slaps down a big bowl of white mush with steam rising out of it and smaller bowls of what looks like snot, with little green flakes and stiff bits of fish floating in it. You have to use your left hand to roll the white mush (*gari*) into a gooey little ball which you dip into the peppery green snot and swallow whole. Then you try not to choke as the hot slippery ball of mush slithers down your throat and lands heavily in the pit of your stomach. I am desperate to have something in my mouth that feels and smells and tastes like home.

I watch Aunty Nneka, my mother's youngest sister, as she turns a page in her book.

'Aunty Nneka,' I say, trembling slightly. 'I'm really terribly sorry to ask. But . . . is there any . . . normal food?'

Agnes laughs and her laugh sounds dry and full of spite.

Aunty Nneka looks up from her book and calls the house-girl, 'English food,' she says. 'Bring Anita some English food.'

Agnes rolls her eyes.

'Every time you talk,' says Anita-Yes. 'Your voice sounds like a white person's.'

Agnes laughs.

'So what?' says Aunty Onyi. 'You could learn something from her. Her voice sounds beautiful.'

A few minutes later, the house-girl, Patty, undulates into the parlour, holding a plate on the palm of her outstretched hand as if she's a waitress in a restaurant. Patty puts the plate down in front of me with no comment. Two fried eggs are sweating oil onto the brown plate.

For a while, no one says anything and I feel sure that my aunties and my sister and Precious-Yes are disappointed in me for asking for the normal food. The room has turned so quiet that I can hear the frogs croaking outside the window. The squelching sound the egg white makes as I mash it between my teeth seems horribly loud.

'I remember when you came before, when you were one small-small girl,' says Aunty Nneka, shielding her eyes from the sun with her hand. 'You're a lot more sociable since then. You don't start crying every time another black person talks to you like you did then.'

Agnes laughs her spiteful laugh again and I glare at her.

Precious-Yes wolfs down the scraps of fried egg that I can't finish. The room stinks of egg and hot pepper and palm oil. A lukewarm early evening breeze blows in through the window, flicking the pages of Aunty Nneka's paperback and making her purse her lips.

I've been told Aunty Nneka is the most intelligent person in the whole family. She doesn't look much like the rest of us; she has a long nose and her face is light brown and long and thin, like one of the cashew nuts that grow in front of the house. She's taller than a man and she has this look of really serious concentration on her face all of the time, even when she's doing nothing more important than leaning back in her wicker rocking chair, sipping lukewarm Fanta.

'I have been given instructions from your mother,' Aunty Nneka says, folding the corner of the page she's reading and shutting her book. 'The travelling musicians are coming soon and Agnes has permission to take you to see them.'

'We are all going to have so much fun!' says Aunty Onyi.

Men with glistening bodies and painted white patterns on their faces glide over to us, making me leap back and suck in a scream. Some of the men carry small drums; others dance, with such bounce in their steps you'd think they were dancing on a trampoline. The tallest of the dancing men stops right in front of me and suddenly opens his mouth into a huge O, as if he's in terrible pain.

There's a bale of straw hanging from the tall dancer's head and more straw wrapped around his legs. I can smell the sweat running down the groove in the centre of his chest. The man lunges forward as if he's going to grab me but instead he hops back. He keeps lunging forward and dancing back again as the straw around his legs shakes and shudders. I gaze into his eyes until I feel dizzy, lose my balance and fall into Agnes's arms.

Agnes sits me down on a log that's propped against a tall thick tree and makes me take deep breaths as she holds my hand and smooths down my dress. Although we're sitting on a dirty old log, both of us are dressed in our very best clothes. I'm wearing a white, frilly, itchy party dress from Harrods that makes me look like a very small bride. I have a hairdo that Patty, the house-girl, did on me that's called threading. Little bunches of hair all over my head were rubbed down with hair grease and wrapped tight with black cotton thread. Now I have thick coils of hair standing away from my head like shiny black antennae.

Agnes is lit up now and again the flickering light cast by the bonfire that the men are dancing around. In the orange firelight, Agnes's nose looks a bit like a toad: squat and brown with tiny bumps all over it, but still she looks beautiful. Her hair is corn-rowed back from her shiny face. She's wearing a red-and-purple dress with very wide shoulders and white embroidery down the front. Agnes sits down next to me on the log and starts rolling her shoulders in time to the singing and drumming.

'I used to belong to a dance troupe when I was little like you, doing native dance,' she says. 'But we didn't know anything about magic like those men.'

I imagine Agnes as a little girl with bales of straw around her legs and on her head, leaping up and down.

'You have to keep your distance from those travelling musicians, you know,' she says. 'If you get too close to them; if you look any of them directly in the eye, then you've had it!'

'What exactly do they do to you?'

'They charm you,' says Agnes. 'They get inside your blood; you become enchanted and you can never be the same again. You start wanting to roam from place to place, just like they do.'

'What if you only look at them for one second?'

'I don't know, Anita,' she says, stretching. 'It's so beautiful here, isn't it? Being here with you reminds me of when I first met you and I begged Mum to let me come to England and be with you.'

'Why did you like me? I thought I was horrible to everyone and kept saying "no" all the time.'

'You're my sister,' Agnes squeezes my hand. 'How does it feel for you to come home?'

'This *isn't* my home,' I reply.

But as soon as I've said these words, I begin to doubt them. Maybe this *is* my home. I do miss Nanny and Gramps and Aunty Wendy and Uncle Mick; I do think about them every day. I miss them the way I miss my favourite characters in a brilliant novel once I've reached the last page, when I'm forced to admit I don't quite live in their world anymore.

And when I was in Fernmere, the place I have always called home, I always had the unsettling feeling that I was sort of living on borrowed time, that I wasn't really supposed to be there. But here, in Chukaro, the days slip by. I've no clear idea how long I've been here. Even my mother's disappearances don't feel confusing because she's just one of an entire sea of family members here.

All of us here: family. With our matching wide cheeks and narrow chins and long legs and short bodies. I'm fussed over more than ever before in my life but I'm not special or different; I'm no longer a circus freak. Chukaro and everyone and everything in it, even the frogs and lizards, belongs to me and maybe I, too, belong to them.

But I also feel like a traitor. What kind of girl would shed Aunty Wendy and Nanny and Uncle Mick like they were crappy old clothes that no longer fit? I feel guilty for enjoying myself so much here: I was supposed to hate it. After all, I'm a British girl, aren't I? Isn't that what Nanny's always told me? I'm just like all the other nice little British girls in Fernmere. That's what Nanny says. That's what Aunty Wendy says.

'So you hate it here then?' says Agnes, breaking into my thoughts.

'No, I like being here. But I . . . I mean; don't you miss being English. Don't you miss Nanny and everyone else?'

'Not really,' says Agnes.

I lean back against the tree trunk. Even with the dancers' drumbeats in the distance, it is so quiet here that I can hear the *zzz* of insects rubbing their legs against their bodies and a sort of whirring noise coming from inside the tree trunk itself.

'Can you hear that, Agnes? There's something crawling around inside this tree. I can hear it.'

'Bloomin' heck! Let's get out of here. Let's go. It's getting late anyway.'

Agnes can't wait to get home and I know why: she's meeting a boy called Duro in the woods behind our grandmother's compound, at eleven o'clock sharp. She has completely forgotten skinny Barry.

Walking home, we can't quite see where we're going. If Agnes didn't know the way by heart, I'd fear we'd just be walking in circles.

'Agnes? Do you think I could tell you a secret?'

'I don't know? Could you?' Agnes's laughter rings out in the darkness like a tinkling bell. 'What secret could *you* have? You're a little girl.

'Here, take this,' she continues.

She hands me two pieces of *akara*, the crunchy greasy balls that are made, I think, from fried beans. To my surprise they taste delicious. I ask for another one. Agnes doesn't give me one, she looks at me and what I can see of her expression in the moonlight is deadly serious.

'What is it, Anita?' she says.

'If I tell you do you promise you won't stop wanting to have me as your sister?'

'You're crying,' Aggy says, draping her warm arm around me.

I feel her fingers tugging playfully at one of the antennae on my head.

'Go on,' she says.

'When I was little . . . these men . . .' I say, feeling that I am about to choke. 'These men, they used to do things to me that made me hurt *down there*. And one of them, he went to the wee-wee in my mouth . . .'

Agnes stops and turns around to face me in the dark, so suddenly that I almost walk straight into her. I feel the *akara* sinking into my stomach.

'I keep having nightmares, Agnes. Where the men come back again.'

'Why didn't you talk to me about it before, Anita?'

'I – I didn't know what to say.'

I am seeing myself as I was when I last remember it happening. Alone in a room at my mother's house in London. Behind a closed door. Footsteps. A man's laughter. A door opening. My knickers being pulled down. More laughter. Feeling like my skin is being peeled off from the inside. Later, walking with my legs very far apart, like a cowboy in a Western.

'I'm really sorry, Anita,' Agnes says. She grabs my hand and we keep walking.

An insect lands on my wrist and starts inching up my arm. I slap it away.

'Anita, listen to me,' she says. 'All you need to do is just forget about what happened to you, OK? Put it out of your mind. Don't ever think about it again after tonight. OK?'

Agnes and I walk through the darkness towards our grandmother's house, holding hands and saying nothing. I whisper 'thank you' but I'm unsure what I'm thanking her for.

It turns out that my revelation wasn't news to Agnes; she'd witnessed what she'd called an 'incident' between me and one of my mother's male friends, years ago. I was a few weeks away from turning four. I don't remember Agnes being there. All I remember about this particular man is him being fat. That he kept perspiring and that he must have been rich because he handed me pocket money afterwards: a twenty-pound note that smelled brand new. Agnes had tried, without success, to protect me.

I uncover this information as an adult, when I gain access to my childhood Social Services records. I find that my then social worker had written and filed away a short report about what happened:

5.6.1975

Mrs Taylor had requested a visit especially as a result of information that Agnes had given her. Agnes is Anita's half-sister and when they were last at home [with their mother] on a weekend together, Agnes was concerned about incidents that occurred with Anita and a man that visited her mother.

Mrs Taylor then said that Anita had complained of vulval soreness and irritation and that when her own daughter, Mrs Travis, had bathed Anita, she had put some cream on that area and thought that Anita was different in some way.

I explained to Mrs Taylor that it was very doubtful if a doctor would be prepared to examine such a small child internally, but I suggested that she might take Anita to her GP for some treatment for the soreness and if the occasion arose, she could then tell him what she suspected.

I suggested to Mrs Taylor that she should endeavour to let Agnes feel that she could talk to her freely about anything for the child had obviously been very bothered by it, to mention it to Mrs Taylor on her return.

I sit in dirt that's as bright as the skin of a clementine. Ants, fat and glossy like black beads, crawl all over my legs and I don't even care. At home, in Fernmere, I see creepy crawly things and I run screaming at the sight of a single ant, the tiniest spider. Here, I am me and an ant is an ant and 'Hideous Africa' is not in the slightest bit hideous.

'What are you doing all by yourself, Precious-No?' says Aunty

Nneka. The bones in her knees creak as she crouches down beside me. 'I'm going to tell you a story,' she says.

The best-ever stories are told in Africa, and Aunty Nneka is the best-ever storyteller. She speaks of something called an *mbari* house where the village's craftsmen congregate to carve sculptures in an orgy of artistry that they offer up to native African gods. Once the gods have feasted their eyes on all the art, the craftsmen destroy it all – and go on to rebuild it again when the gods need soothing next time.

African gods? I just can't believe it. I've heard of Greek gods. I've seen pictures in my illustrated children's Bible of the English god who I thought was everyone's god: a white man in a white robe with a long white beard.

'Are the gods coloured, Aunty? Is their skin brown like ours?'

'Gods don't have skins,' says Aunty Nneka.

We sit in silence.

'I can feel your mind whirring,' Aunty Nneka says, finally. 'What are you thinking about?'

'How come I don't live with my real family all the time, Aunty?'

'It's just the way things are. Right now.'

'But there must be a reason.'

'Everything is everything.'

This new phrase crawls into my head and my mind goes round and round trying to understand it.

'Is that a riddle? What does that mean, Aunty?'

'It means that everything in this minute is exactly as it is meant to be.'

I begin to count. One-plus-two-plus-three. All the way up to sixty.

'It's a new minute now, Aunty. Is everything still everything?'

'Everything is as it's meant to be in *every* minute.'

On Christmas Eve, I begin seeing things that other people say are not real.

The day starts as normally as a Christmas Eve spent in Africa can: I wake up covered in sweat and fresh mosquito bites. When I climb out of my grandmother's bed, it is so early that night hasn't quite given way to morning and the sky outside is still dark and bluish-purple, like a bruise. I trot through the small house and slip noiselessly into the steaming-hot kitchen where I stand in a corner, watching Patty do her chores.

Patty has a rhythm going. She leans over the table holding a big rusty knife and begins chopping up something I can't quite see and every few minutes she stops, cocks her head to one side, looks out of the window and leans forward and starts chopping again. Finally, she turns around and screams.

'Anita! You scared me-oh! I didn't hear you come in!'

As soon as Patty sees me, she starts spooning bright orange palm oil into a big brown frying pan. She grabs two ripe plantains and yanks their skins off. She slits the yellow flesh into thin slices with her knife, sprinkles the slices with salt and flings them into the frying pan.

Patty fries plantain pretty much every time she catches sight of me. Now that she's found African food that I will actually eat, she seems pleased, or relieved.

'Eat,' she says, putting a plate piled high with sweet, crisp plantain on the table in front of me.

As I munch plantain, Agnes strides into the kitchen, carrying what looks like a gigantic knobbly bar of soap. She drops this bar of soap – which is about three feet long – onto the kitchen table and it lands with a gentle thud on top of the plantain skins and chopped onions.

'I made this myself,' Agnes says.

'Wow!' I say. 'How did you make it?'

'Palm oil; lye,' she says, cutting off chunks of soap and placing them into a large basket. 'I'm going to try to sell it at the market today and make *naira* to buy Christmas presents with. Want to come and help me sell it?'

'Will you give me my own bar of soap if I help you?'

'I've got something better for you. Aunty Edna already gave me some traditional soap she said I should give to you; it will help your eczema. Wait, yeah?'

Agnes disappears into the back of the house, comes back and drops a brownish black squidgy lump with white specks in it into my hand.

'I don't know how to make the traditional soap yet. It's made with cocoa leaves and paw-paw and all that,' Agnes says, cramming a slice of plantain into her mouth. 'Go and wash and get dressed. We need to get to the market early.'

We arrive at the market, and as we stroll through it, I feel suffocated by the smell of raw animal flesh mingled with decaying fish that fills the breeze-less morning air. I've been to the market in Chichester before, where local gypsies hawk dodgy kitchen appliances, knock-off perfume and bruised-looking fruit and veg. But nothing has prepared me for the explosion of colour and noise and the stomach-churning stench of this market in Chukaro.

Searching for a spot in the shade where we can sell our soap, Agnes and I pass rickety tables laid out with sinister-looking things to eat. There are dried bats that look like dusty black leather gloves and whole fishes that are so old they feel like cardboard when I poke at them.

Standing on a table, at the centre of a circle of ladies who are screaming, 'How much? Give me, give me!' is a goat. The goat's skin has been torn off and blood drips from its raw pink flesh. The goat's head lies next to it on the table, crawling with fat, brightly coloured flies. Agnes stops to examine the goat's head and tells me about the delicious soup our grandmother could make with it. I shiver.

Basket of soap in hand, Agnes weaves her way through the crowd with her nose in the air, looking so snooty that I bet people think she could buy up the entire market if she felt like it. Maybe Agnes really *could* buy the whole market; she's got a purse stuffed full of pound notes, after all. People in Africa go crazy for pound notes. When I was introduced to my great-aunt Edna, the first – and only – thing she said to me was, 'Did you bring me British pounds-oh? Did you bring me US dollars, I beg?'

'Let me buy you a nice cold Fanta,' says Agnes. 'Or you can have a Coke if you want.'

'Can I really, Agnes?' I say, shocked. I am not allowed Coke at home. Nanny says it turns your blood to poison.

I draw my shoulders back, copying Agnes's self-possessed walk, and we push past other shoppers and sellers to get to the lady selling cold drinks. A red motorbike whizzes past us, making red dust fly up all around us and narrowly misses Agnes's left shoulder.

As I turn to watch the motorbike speed off, I notice that I'm being watched by a boy about the same age as me who is trailing dreamily behind a very thin woman with white hair. The boy is wearing a brown shirt that's hanging off his body revealing a belly button that pokes out a long way, like Pinocchio's nose. The annoyed-looking woman reaches out her hand to the boy but he's too busy looking at me to catch up with her.

The man on the motorbike swoops past again, but this time he catches the little boy's shirt in the motorbike's handlebars. I watch as the boy is dragged slowly towards the ground where his skull slams against one of the motorbike's wheels. There is a series of thuds as the basket of vegetables the woman was carrying falls to the ground and then she herself falls to her knees in the orange dust, screaming and screaming. The boy's head is laid to the side, his cheek resting against the earth. Thick, raspberry-red liquid oozes from the enormous split that runs from the nape of his neck to the crown of his head and onto the earth.

In slow-motion, feeling somehow as though I'm trying to run underwater, I fall onto my trembling knees and cover my temples with the palms of my hands and scream, OH MY GOD! OH MY GOD! OH MY GOD!

Agnes yanks my arm. 'What on earth is wrong, Anita? Get up!'

'Don't you care about that poor boy? I think he's dead.'

'What boy? This isn't funny, Anita; what are you going on about? I think the heat has got to you,' says Agnes, trying to drag me to my feet. 'No: I think you are actually going mad. I'm not joking, Anita. There's a lot of madness in our family.'

'Don't touch me!' I scream.

'In all seriousness, you have gone mad,' says Agnes, shaking her head.

I am lying on my grandmother's bed with a sheet wrapped tightly around me, wondering how going mad will change my life. I feel trapped and uncomfortable: my tightly threaded hairdo won't let me rest my head against the pillow and whatever position I lie in hurts.

I hear something that sounds like paper rustling and I spring from the pillow, feel my weird antenna hair standing up, and look around me. My grandmother is standing in the shadows in the corner of the bedroom, turning the pages of a thick white Bible. She sees me and walks slowly over to the bed and sits on the edge of it. She lays the Bible in my lap and smiles.

'I love God very much,' my grandmother says, in perfect English.

Holding her yellow wrapper up above her knees, she climbs onto the end of the bed and stands there, peering down at me. Her hairy legs are dotted with dark brown scars that were left behind by vicious mosquitoes.

'Anita, you didn't know I could speak English did you?' she says.

In one smooth movement, my grandmother hops from one end of the bed to the other. She lands close to my head, with one bare foot on the pillow and the other foot balancing behind her in the air.

'I bet you didn't know I could jump like that, either, did you? I can do anything I want to,' she says. 'And no one can stop me.'

My grandmother's yellow headscarf slides off her head onto

the floor, revealing hair which is long and threaded in the same style as mine. She runs a honey-brown hand through her hair and down the side of her face to her neck.

'Feel how soft my skin still is,' my grandmother says, pushing her face towards mine. I reach my hand up to touch her skin and find that there's nothing there but thin air.

'Put your tongue out,' someone whispers. 'Open your mouth!'

'No!' I shout. 'No!'

I feel rage boil inside me. I will not accept any more filthy nastiness into my mouth. I will stand up for myself. I will push away the body behind this whispering voice that's telling me to open up. If this is madness, I thank the African gods for it because madness has opened my eyes and loosened my tongue.

'No!'

I struggle to sit up.

'Anita, do as you're told. Please.' It is Mummy Elizabeth's voice. She places her hand in mine.

Gingerly, I poke out my tongue and feel drops of liquid slowly falling onto it. I open my eyes and see my mother hovering over me holding a plastic beaker to my lips. Her face is shining with sweat. I touch my mother's face and this startles her, making her drip some of the water from the beaker onto my burning throat. She dabs the water away with a corner of the bed sheet.

'You're very, very sick,' my mother says.

'No, I'm not,' I say, sitting bolt upright. 'Agnes told me I might be going mad but I think she was just being spiteful and I think I just had a nightmare, that's all.'

'You look terrible. Terrible,' my mother says. 'I'm sending for the doctor.'

Within minutes of being sent for, the doctor waddles in: monstrously fat, damp with sweat and carrying a bulging black leather bag.

'Are you my godfather?' I ask the doctor. It comes out as 'good-father'. 'My mother said my godfather's a doctor.'

The doctor laughs, making a whirring noise that sounds like wahwahwah. I cringe and stare up at the wobbling layers of flab beneath his chin.

'Well,' he says. 'You could say that I'm a good friend of your mother's.'

The doctor's light brown face has a slimy and raw look to it, making me think of a snail without a shell. In his high, girlish voice he asks me question after question until I start feeling woozy. Unable to look at him any more, I close my eyes.

The doctor's voice is pleasingly, disarmingly un-scary, like a woman's. My mother holds my hand. I flush with pleasure. My mother, the brilliant elusive hummingbird, has flitted to my side. Feeling her fingers interlaced so tightly with mine makes me feel that whatever the doctor says is wrong with me, I'm ultimately going to be all right. I squeeze my mother's hand.

'Have you been bitten a lot?' the doctor asks.

'Bitten by what?' I murmur in a croaky voice. 'A tiger?'

He laughs again: wahwahwah.

'Mosquitoes!' says the doctor. 'In a way, we have a lot to thank mosquitoes for. Without them we'd never have got our independence: it's the mosquitoes that finally drove the white man out of Nigeria. We should have an image of a mosquito in our national flag, don't you think? How are you feeling? Where does it pain you?'

'My tummy hurts.'

Using his fat fingers and the palms of his sweaty hands, the doctor presses down on my stomach, the same way you'd press the top of an apple pie you were about to shove into the oven. I flinch and begin to cry.

Each time he asks, 'Does it hurt here? Or here?' I nod. Everything hurts. My brain and even my heart hurts.

The doctor pushes a thermometer into my mouth and I gag

and hold my breath. My fingernails dig into my mother's hands. The doctor takes my hand and presses his thumb into my wrist for a minute or two and opens his black bag.

'She must take these,' he says to my mother, dropping a white envelope of pills into her hand. 'This child almost certainly has malaria.'

BOOK TWO

'But I don't want to go among mad people,' said Alice. 'Oh, you can't help that,' said the cat. 'We're all mad here.'

Lewis Carroll,
Alice's Adventures in Wonderland

The Bowler Hat Collector

'STILL GETTING CHILLS, darling?' says Nanny.

'Yes,' I lie.

I've been off school for weeks, supposedly near-death as a result of the malaria. Nanny has moved me into her bedroom so that she can keep an eye on me during the night. I sleep in the twin divan that was once Gramps's. Aggy's back too. She's back in the box room and has even less to do with us than ever.

'It was awful for Anita,' Nanny tells my form teacher on the phone. 'Thank God we got her home in the nick of time.'

How is Nanny responsible for getting me home? It's not as if she paid for my return plane ticket, and I do not believe my real family nearly let me die.

I have been waiting and waiting for a chance to tell somebody my stories from Nigeria. I have wanted to tell Nanny and Aunty Wendy about Chukaro and what I did there and what the people I met there were like. I try to spark up conversations about the family I met in Chukaro, about the ancestors I learned of who now feel like living people to me.

I want to tell Nanny all about the dusty old book called My Africa that my Aunty showed me and about the terrifying photo of my great-grandfather's body printed inside the book, and about the epitaph beneath the photo: 'Here lies King Eze Uche, the shrewdest politician I ever knew.'

Nobody asks.

'Did you know black people could be kings, Nanny?' I say one day.

'You know we don't use the word "black", Nin,' she says, and dashes off to get my lunch ready.

I am black now, actually. Since Nigeria, I've ceased being coloured. Aunty Nneka explained to me that only racist whites call us coloured now and we must never use that word to describe ourselves.

Back in Fernmere it is hard to continue to see being black as a good thing though. I test my new way of looking at myself on Aunty Wendy and Nanny. On the way to Sainsbury's in Chichester in the car I say, 'Guess what?'

'What, love?' says Nanny.

'I'm black and I'm proud!' I say, copying words I've seen a bouffant-haired, dancing black man say on TV. I giggle nervously.

Nanny turns round and look at me as though I've just announced that I am Lucifer. She stops chewing her little Scotch egg, her mouth drops open ever so slightly, and I can see the mashed up pink and yellow and white inside.

One winter afternoon, while I'm still off school, I am woken from a snooze by the sound of a human trying to imitate a cuckoo at the front door downstairs: it's Aunty Wendy. Suddenly I hear Aunty Wendy actually *running* up the stairs.

Aunty Wendy sits on the edge of Gramps's bed with such bounce that she almost lands on top of me. 'Don't you feel like getting up and going out for a bit of a walk? Get some fresh air, love?' she says. 'Can't be doing you no good just lying there like an invalid.'

'No,' I say.

Nanny, who is perched at her dressing table, tweezing at a hair on her chin, turns around and smiles at us.

'Are you going to tell her or shall I, Wendy?' she says

Looking at Aunty Wendy's lit-up face I can see what she must have looked like when she was my age.

'You tell her, Mum.'

'What?' I say. 'I mean, *pardon?*'

'Wendy's having a little baby of her own, Nin. Isn't it wonderful?' says Nanny.

Aunty Wendy squeezes my hand tight.

At the end of the month, I finally return to Fernmere Primary and kids who've never so much as said hello to me before, come up to me on the playground and go, 'Hi. How's it going?'

Later I learn from a new kid in my class, Tom, that our headmaster told everyone to be kind to me when I came back, since I'd been through an 'ordeal'. I revel in my new-found fame and wish I could have malaria more often.

A few weeks later, my mother struts back into my life to take me up to London for the weekend, and I'm thrilled to see her. I've been feeling so threatened by this white baby that's growing in Aunty Wendy's tummy that I feel relieved to have my own mother, however flawed and unpredictable she might be.

According to Nanny my mother is behind with her payments for my keep, but she surprises us all by giving me a cheque for a hundred pounds.

'To put in your building society account,' my mother says.

After thanking her, I fold the cheque in half and tuck it into my pink plastic handbag. My mother says that her car has gone and when I ask her where it went, she doesn't answer me. We're on the train. My mother whispers into my ear that there is going to be a surprise for me in London and that the surprise is a person.

'It's somebody I want you to meet,' she says.

'Give me a clue. Man or lady?'

'Oh, it's a man.'

I think of the man holding me in the Polaroid I found long ago at my mother's house; the man with the small teeth who I've always thought was my father. I've never dared ask my mother about this man because I came across the Polaroid one day when she went out when, out of boredom, I rummaged through three of the animal-hide handbags she kept in the bottom of her wardrobe.

My mother has never seemed to want me to meet or know anything about my father. Nanny once helped me write a letter to the Sierra Leonian High Commission, enclosing a copy of my birth certificate and asking them to help us locate him, but we didn't hear back.

When I do eventually trace my father, more than twenty years from now, I will be informed that I have missed him by three years. He was shot in the chest during the Sierra Leonean civil war in 1999.

'Can you give me another clue, Mummy? What sort of teeth does the person have?'

My mother ignores the question but doesn't appear annoyed that I asked it. She sweeps one of her long arms around my shoulder and presses my face up against her cheek.

'You're a blessing to me, do you know that?' she says, nuzzling her nose into my cheekbone.

I nod, not because I understand what my mother really means, but because I think she's expecting me to nod.

'I'm going to try to be a better mother to you from now on. Tell me some nice things you'd like to do with the rest of the day. Your choice.'

'Do they have libraries in London, Mum?'

'Libraries? I mean something fun. Like the pictures or shopping.'

I watch her, not quite trusting her. If I do anything that's even the slightest bit annoying, I know there's a good chance she'll explode.

But I never know when she's going to totally lose it with me and starting punching or kicking me again. It may never happen again, or it may happen five seconds from now, and that's the horror of it.

But when we arrive in London, my mother's still in a light-hearted mood. We drift from shop to shop and my mother buys a lot of things on each floor of each shop; lip glosses, glitter pens, a gold bangle, five bottles of body lotion, nail varnish and rings. She doesn't say whether these things are for me, for her or for somebody else. I get swept up in the euphoria of her spending and assume everything's for me – although later I find out that only the glitter pens were bought with me in mind. When it's time to pay my mother hands over a plastic card that the check-out girls slide inside a metal machine and hand back to her with a big white receipt, smiling.

Later, in Selfridges, my mother buys me a jacket made of brown leather and rabbit fur. It's too big for me but she tells me to put it on, there and then, over my anorak. The jacket reaches my knees and I stand there, rubbing my chin against the fur and smiling bravely at my mother, trying not to think of the blood-soaked bunnies who lost their lives so that I could wear this jacket.

'Don't let that foolish Nanny put it in the washing machine,' says my mother.

We leave Selfridges just as it's about to close. Laden with shopping bags, we battle our way along a very wide pavement that's clogged up with people pushing and shoving and carrying three or more carrier bags each. My mother gestures towards a grand-looking hotel that's tucked along a side street between Selfridges and Marble Arch tube station.

'I used to live inside there when I first came to London,' she says.

'You lived inside a hotel? How come?'

'Where else would you expect me to live? You think any white person taking one look at my black face or hearing my African name or my accent, you think they'd rent to me?'

Isn't her name, the name she uses most often, Elizabeth Williams? How African is that?

'Your name's not really African though, is it, Mummy?'

'My *African* name,' my mother says. 'Oluchi Eze. I already told you. Remember?' I nod.

'What's *my* African name?'

'The last thing I'd want to do is hinder you with some kind of Third World name,' my mother says. 'You don't have any such thing.'

'Has Agnes got an African name?'

'That Agnes's got an African *everything*. That girl,' my mother says, 'that girl is just like any girl from back home in the village. It's like she never left there and lived in England. You wouldn't even know she goes to school. I'm telling you! Education is wasted on her.'

Seven a.m. I've been with my mother exactly sixteen hours and she hasn't blown her top once. She hasn't hit me or even raised her voice and she hasn't buggered off and left me on my own either because I can hear her laughter floating up from the dining room.

I climb out of bed, retrieve my cheque for a hundred pounds from beneath my pillow and tuck it into my dressing-gown pocket. I have a rummage through the drawers in the dressing table opposite my bed. Nanny's instructed me to find out whether my mother has any DHSS child benefit books lying around (I find two of them) and how much money she's got in her building society account. I'm unable to find a building society passbook anywhere, so I've nothing to report to Nanny on that front. I've no idea why Nanny wants to know and I don't ask.

Feeling guilty for snooping, I close the drawers. I open my little suitcase and take out my sketchpad, rip a page out of my sketchpad, fold it in half and draw a picture of a brown woman sporting a big red smile and a huge red outline of a heart on her chest. I draw the letter M inside the heart. Inside the folded page, using my new silver glitter pen, I write the words I LOVE YOU arranged in a rainbow shape, around the woman's head.

I put on my dressing gown and leave it unbuttoned so that it floats behind me as I walk in the exact same way I've seen my mother walk, with her dressing gown float behind her. I descend the stairs preparing what I'm going to say, whispering aloud, concentrating very hard; mornings at my mother's can be complicated. It can be a bit tricky to get everything right and I have to remember to not just say 'Hi' or 'Good morning' when I first encounter my mother in the morning: I must say, 'Good-morning-mummy-did-you-sleep-well-can-I-make-you-a-cup-of-tea?' My mother has spent a lot of energy teaching me this.

On the dining table there are three plates of toast cut into triangles, smeared with my favourite grapefruit marmalade. And sitting opposite my mother is a man, a man with very wide dark brown cheeks and a pointed chin. Although he is sitting down, big thighs splayed, I can tell that he's very short for a grown-up, barely taller than me.

I keep my eyes on the man as I hand my mother the card I just made. 'This is for you. The "M" inside the heart is for mother.'

I feel like a moron giving her the card while the short man watches me but he just smiles as though he's impressed and my mother smiles too. She's wearing shimmering burgundy lipstick, even though it's not quite eight o'clock in the morning.

In a slightly shaky voice I offer to make my mother and the man a cup of tea but they say no thanks. I sit down and bite into a triangle of toast and wait for an explanation as to who the man is and what he's doing at my mother's dining table.

'This is Uncle Abejide,' my mother says finally. 'He's my fiancé.'

'Neety,' Uncle Abejide says, in a voice that would make you think he actually knew me. 'Your mother tells me you're very brilliant.'

He grins. He has very uniform white teeth, this man. All of Mother's boyfriends have had lovely teeth and smile a lot. But that doesn't mean I can trust them. This man can smile at me all he wants, I will not drop my guard when he's present.

I smile nervously, giggle a little, and look down at my plate.

'Answer him!' my mother says, drawing in breath sharply, sounding like she's rapidly running out of patience with me.

'Um, thank you, Uncle Abby.'

'Drink up your Horlicks,' my mother says.

After he's gobbled up most of the toast, Uncle Abejide says, 'Well, I must be going.'

He hops up and puts a black bowler hat on his head and twists the brim around a little and makes a big show of bowing down to kiss me on the cheek. The hat makes his face look even wider. 'I'll see you again, Neety,' he says.

My mother helps him into a long, stiff-looking black coat and he takes her into his arms and kisses her, keeping his lips on hers for a long time. I wonder what sort of Valentine's card he gave her and whether he bought her flowers too. The door closes and my mother puts the chain up.

'He's crazy about bowler hats,' she says, smiling. 'He collects them.'

'That's nice. Is Uncle Abba-thingie my real father? Is that how come you're getting married to him?'

'Don't start *this* up again.'

I lean back in my chair and stretch, pretending not to feel disappointed. 'What are we going to do today, Mummy?'

'We'll start,' my mother says, 'by clearing these dishes.'

I follow her into the kitchen.

'I remember when you were three or four,' she says, grinning, 'and you were so sweet that you tried to do the washing up for me because you didn't want me to ruin my hands. You said, "But *I* want to do it mummy." But you were so small that you couldn't even reach as high as the kitchen sink!'

'Aww,' I say, enjoying this image and the fact that it seems to soften and amuse my mother.

The kitchen sink is filled with large plates and there's an oily orangey-red film floating on top of the water. I put the plates and knives that I'm carrying on the sideboard next to the bread bin. Through the kitchen window I can see Cynthia and another girl, both in powder-blue anoraks, playing some kind of skipping game out on the pavement.

'Would you mind if I go outside and play, Mum?'

I want to escape my mother's gaze for a while, so that I can take a bite out of this idea of her getting married and chew it over in private. I'm the child; I'm the one who's supposed to be constantly changing but suddenly it's the grown-ups around me who are growing, changing, making babies, getting married, stirring up excitement among themselves and I don't like it. I need to come up with a strategy to prevent more change from happening.

'And is it all right if I go and find a sweet shop as well?'

From out of nowhere, my mother's palm lands with a crack against my cheekbone, propelling me backwards. I smash into the fridge-freezer behind me and the fridge's handle digs into the place where my spine meets the bottom of my neck. I begin trembling, literally vibrating; partly from the impact of my mother's punch but mainly I am shaking with anger.

'Who do you expect to do all this washing up?' my mother screams, stalking towards me with her finger pointed at my face, her face drained of all affection for me.

I close my eyes, turn my head away and reach my hand over my shoulder and inside my pyjama top to see whether my back is bleeding. It isn't.

'Just leaving the plates there like that,' my mother continues, furiously turning on the kitchen taps. 'Who exactly do you think you are? Who do I have here to help me with the housework? Do you see any house-girl here? You are my child, you should be helping me, not pissing me off!'

I touch my swelling cheek with the tips of my fingers. 'I wasn't thinking,' I say. 'I'm really sorry, Mummy.'

But I am not sorry. Not at all. My mother has pushed me over an invisible edge. I am vibrant with rage: a cauldron of anger and hate is cooking inside me. I desperately want to hit my mother back, smash her against the fridge and humiliate her; force her to know how it feels to be bullied. Soon, I think. Soon. I simmer, and wait.

I feel her eyes boring into my back as I tiptoe across the room to the sideboard, pick up the small stack of plates and cups I left there and lay them gently on top of the dishes already filling the sink. I think: I'm not going to let her get away with this.

My mother doesn't believe kids should be seen and not heard; she believes they should be neither seen nor heard. So it's strange when she asks me if I want to accompany her to a grown-ups' party that she says she's been looking forward to all week. It's my mother's way of saying sorry for hitting me, I think. But I'm not impressed.

'If you don't want to come to the party, you can go to the pictures,' she says in a sickeningly gentle voice. 'It's up to you.'

I ask who'll be at the party.

'People from my office,' says my mother.

Boring as grown-ups' parties are, I'm tempted to go so that I can obtain rich gossip for Nanny and Aunty Wendy. They would love to know where my mother works and what sort of people she spends Monday to Friday working with and so, I suppose, would I.

'Would I have to go the pictures all by myself then?' I say curtly, still weighing each option.

'I'll call Patience and tell her to send Eddie to keep you company and take you to the pictures,' my mother says, sounding as though her mind's now made up.

'Isn't he at boarding school?' I say, trying to hold in my interest. If my mother realises I'm excited about seeing him she might decide to take me to the party after all; she seems to get turned on by other people's sadness.

'Eddie got expelled,' my mother says, pouting into her dressing-table mirror.

Eddie arrives in a denim jacket with studs all over it. He's had his Afro cut off which makes his face and his nose look larger than when I first met him.

'What's happenin'?' he says, in a new American accent. 'What have you done to your face?'

I had hoped he'd say: 'I've missed you.'

'I was playing in the garden and I fell over,' I mumble.

I look through the parlour window, into the blackness of the back garden and wonder if the dead rat's still out there, decaying. Maybe it was my mother who actually killed that rat; I imagine her stamping on it until its insides spilled out onto the un-mown grass.

The raw memory of my mother hitting me lingers inside, rendering me thirstier than ever for approval from someone, from anyone. From Eddie.

'I stayed in the US all summer with my aunty,' Eddie says. 'You should see it, man. Everyone has huge cars and the sidewalks are this wide,' he spreads his arms wide.

'What's a sidewalk?' I ask.

'Say what?' he says, clicking his fingers. 'It's a pavement, ain't it?'

'Why did you get expelled from boarding school?' I say.

'What's it to you, babe? What movie are we gonna see? *Quadrophenia*?'

'I doubt we'd get in to see it,' I say. 'We don't look old enough.'

It occurs to me that whether we look old enough or not, we cannot get into the pictures without money. I go upstairs and poke my head around my mother's bedroom door. She is sitting at her dressing table, patting caramel-coloured powder all over her face, grinning at her own reflection. How can somebody so pretty be so unkind? I linger in the doorway watching her, waiting for her to ask me what I want, hoping she'll be able to read my mind so that I won't have to ask her outright for cash.

'Go and play with Eddie,' she says to my reflection.

Before my mother leaves the house, she hands Eddie and me a fifty-pence coin each. 'Remember to eat,' she says. 'I left *gari* and stockfish in the oven for you two. And see a movie that's suitable for children, OK?'

I cannot find the food my mother says she's left for us.

Rifling through her cupboards, I find nothing that looks even vaguely appetising.

'Are you hungry, Eddie?' I call from the kitchen, thinking – hoping – that he's got some pound notes in his pocket. 'There's a Kentucky around the corner. We could go and get some to take away. If you want.'

Eddie's too cool to say yes or no but he says 'maybe' and slips his denim jacket back on.

At the Kentucky Fried Chicken, I grin greedily as we ask for five pieces of chicken each.

'Legs only,' Eddie says. 'No breast.'

The girl dishing up our chicken has dark freckles forming a thick pattern over the top of her face, like a mask. I can't stop looking at it. She slaps a red and white Kentucky Fried Chicken paper bag on top of the counter and I feel ravenously hungry at the sight of the chicken grease that's oozing through the bottom of the bag, turning it translucent. Eddie reaches into his stripy trousers, pulls out the fifty pence my mother gave him and looks at it thoughtfully and he reaches up, grabs the bag from the counter, grabs my hand with his other hand and pulls me through the door. We run down the street, our boxes of chicken bouncing inside the paper bag.

'Did you pay the lady?' I ask breathlessly.

'No.'

We eat our contraband at my mother's house.

'Isn't it wrong to steal?' I say.

Eddie shrugs.

Eddie puts his arm around me and tells me he's missed me.

'Did you go out with anyone else when I wasn't around?' I ask.

'Of course not,' he says immediately.

We talk more about New York and about the black kids Eddie met there who drove their own cars. I tell him about Nigeria and about looking into the eyes of the travelling musicians and how it has left me restless and feeling uprooted and almost ready to run away from home and unsure even of where or with whom my home is these days.

I realise that this is the first time I have given voice to these feelings. I really do feel like a leaf being swept along by the wind. I've no idea what my future holds; where I might end up, whether I'll eventually live in Nigeria or not. What will happen to me if Nanny, who is in her late sixties, should die? What if my mother has new children after she gets married? Will I count? Will I still matter? Why do Aunty Wendy and Uncle Mick need a baby of their own when they already have me? I talk and talk about all of these things until Eddie suddenly yawns. He looks deeply bored. I shut up. Neither of us says anything.

The clock ticking over my mother's marble mantelpiece says eight o'clock. My mother said she'd be back late. Late means after midnight. I know what a boy like Eddie must be thinking right now: that I'm not cool or interesting enough to be worthy of his time. What if he stills see the dull me; the drab, timid little girl who used to call herself coloured? It may be only a matter of minutes, before Eddie decides that I'm nothing special.

Silence.

I search my mind for something that might hold Eddie's interest. I find it.

'Umm. Would you like me to do something?'

'Go on, then.'

I kneel on the porridge-coloured carpet and feel my knees sink into its softness. Pushing aside the empty fried chicken cartons, I crawl closer to Eddie, open my mouth into a wide O and clamp it on the mound where his thighs meet, feeling movement beneath the heavy cotton of his trousers. I am secretly hoping my mother will walk in and see me and be utterly repulsed and humiliated by what's become of her daughter. I want her to *know*.

I wait. Mouth open, jaw starting to ache.

Eddie smirks and gently strokes my face.

'You've got to take my thing out of my trousers first, ain't it?' he says, stepping back a little and unzipping his flies.

Two weeks later, a letter filled with long words arrives for me from the Gateway building society. I show it to Nanny at the breakfast table. 'That cheque your mother wrote you has bounced,' says Nanny with a flicker of a smirk. 'Either that or she put a stop on it.'

Upside Down

LIFE TURNS EASY AND weeks and months melt happily into one another.

I write a poem about a cat that can read people's minds. I send it into a comic, they publish it and pay me two pounds.

As Aunty Wendy's belly swells, she and Uncle Mick buy me more sweets, more stickers, more Sindy doll's clothes than ever. 'I don't want you feeling left out or nothing,' Uncle Mick says.

My mother doesn't ring or write or turn up, and I don't care since I still hate her.

Then, one afternoon, I emerge from school, laden with library books, and find there's nobody there to meet me. I wait and wait. I walk down the steep little hill to Parkfield Road. No Nanny. No Aunty Wendy. Not even Agnes. I stare wanly at the passing cars, my satchel weighing heavily on my shoulder.

'Wotcha!' A rough male voice. 'Where you off to then?'

Across the road, leaning against someone's garden fence, one skinny leg crossed in front of the other, is Uncle Mick. He is rolling a Rizla between his thumb and forefinger. Uncle Mick's hair billows out in the wind, forming a halo around his thin face. He dips his head and lights his fag.

'What are you doing here?'

I dread hearing the answer to my own question. Uncle Mick should be at work. Him being here means something is seriously wrong. Nanny and Aunty Wendy may be dead. My mother might have killed them.

'Shouldn't you be at work Uncle Mick?'

'Keep your hair on, mate. Got the afternoon off, didn't I?'

'How come?'

'Do you ever stop asking bleeding questions? Like being interrogated being around you. Hurry up then, nipper.'

I try to keep up with Uncle Mick's loping strides.

'Where's Aunty Wendy then?'

'She's up St Richard's hospital, isn't she.'

I stop mid-stride.

'Is she . . . still alive?'

'Of course she's bloody alive! She's having a check-up.'

'Is her baby coming out, Uncle Mick?'

'I should bloody well hope not,' says Uncle Mick, laughing nervously. 'It's not due yet, is it?'

'Where's Nanny?'

'With Wendy. Drove her to the hospital. You gonna stand here talkin' then, or are you coming home?'

We walk through Hunter Close, where some of the poshest kids at my school live. We cross New Road taking the shortcut to Woodview – a narrow path that's sandwiched between the fire station and an explosion of blackberry bushes whose branches tear at your hair as you pass.

'I've been told to tell you your mother's rung for you earlier. You know, you never told me what that Africa was like. Secretive little bugger, ain't you?'

'It was quite a good laugh being there,' I say, smiling up at him. 'Until, you know, I got ill. My cousins and aunties were really nice.'

'So you liked it then? I don't blame you.'

As we walk, I casually search the blackberry bushes for ripe fruit but every blackberry I see is either green and too unripe to eat or brown and all shrivelled up. Somehow Uncle Mick finds one that is deep purple, fat and bursting with sugary juice. He pops the blackberry into my eager mouth and I swallow it without chewing, as if I was a snake.

'That one had a worm inside it, didn't it?' he says laughing.

After we've had our tea and watched *Top of the Pops*, Uncle Mick lets me flick through his record collection.

'I'm teaching myself to become a DJ, aren't I?' he says

'Why?'

'So I can make a bit of money, DJin' at people's parties and weddings and that.'

'Uncle Mick? who's your favourite singer?'

His smile is radiant. 'Who do you think? The Stones! I'd give anything to meet that bloody Mick Jagger.'

We delve into Uncle Mick's stack of records, which is at least twice the size of my mother's record collection. A Diana Ross single called 'Upside Down' falls out of the stack and slides onto the floor of the loft. On the cover of the single is a photo of Diana wearing skin-tight jeans. Her hair's long and wavy and her brown eyes are glossy and enormous. This is how I'd like to look when I'm grown up. Apart from her lips, which are plump and slightly parted; they look wet. Her mouth looks disgusting, I think.

'Nice isn't she? That Diana Ross.'

Not exactly nice, I think. She reminds me of my mother, which means she is scary and beautiful at the same time.

'What's wrong with you?' says Uncle Mick.

I shrug.

'Haven't changed, have you?' he says.

'Since when?'

'Since your mother first brought you. Lovely little kid then you were and you still are, aren't you? But you'll go back one day, won't ya Neety Williams?'

'What do you mean?'

'You'll go back one day. You'll forget all about us lot one day. Won't you? We love you, but you're not ours.'

It is half term. I'm gulping lemonade straight from the can and watching raindrops bounce off a wide white London pavement. Uncle Mick is standing next to me, holding my hand and singing:

'Where are we going? I said: "where are we going?" '

'To the zoo!' I shout.

'We're going to the zoo, zoo, zoo,' he sings. 'How about you, you, you. You can come too, too, too. We're going to the zoo. If we can bloody find it.'

Aunty Wendy looks up from the map she is reading. 'Watch your language, Mick.'

Uncle Mick smirks and sucks on his roll-up cigarette.

When we finally arrive at London Zoo, Uncle Mick looks around, unimpressed.

'They got a lot of these animals where you're from, Neeta. Ha ha ha. They're used to seeing kids that look like you,' he says. 'Ha ha ha, look at that! It'll show us its arse in a minute.'

An apathetic-looking monkey is doing a wee on the ground near the edge of its cage and the animal stink mingles with the smell of clean rainfall and fills the air. We walk away quickly, to the next cage, before the monkey can show us its arse.

'Aren't you gonna say hello to the elephants, Nin?' says Uncle Mick.

Feeling like a moron, I wave at one of the elephants. I look up into the elephant's small, knowing eyes set deep into its huge wrinkly old head. The elephant looks down at me as though I am not even as important as a fly. I imagine its huge crusty foot crushing me into the damp ground and no one even noticing.

Looking at Aunty Wendy's huge belly, I wonder if my life will change once her little baby's born. How can I be one hundred per cent sure I won't get forgotten? Sent back to where I came from? Or worse, because Mummy Elizabeth doesn't seem to really want me, I'll be sent to the children's home in Cocking, where – I've heard – they feed you rank food that makes you puke and then they make you eat your own sick.

The caged animals seem sulky and they are nowhere near as exciting to me as Uncle Mick is as he drifts around the zoo, poking his fingers through dangerous animals' cages and throwing his frizzy head back, laughing.

'Mick, that thing could take your hand clean off,' says Aunty Wendy.

Uncle Mick says, 'And why do you think I'd give a toss if it did?'

I clutch Uncle Mick's hand. I don't want this day, this moment, to ever end.

It's Aunty Wendy who has the idea of phoning up my mother – since we're already in London – and inviting ourselves round for a cup of tea.

'Why would she want to associate with the likes of us?' Uncle Mick says, laughing.

Aunty Wendy ignores him. She squeezes her big belly into a phone box that smells of wee, and picks up the receiver.

'What's her new phone number, Neet?' Aunty Wendy says, leaning out the door of the phone box.

'I don't know.'

'What's her new address then, love?'

'It's number nineteen.'

'Number nineteen what, love? What's the name of the road?'

I'm ashamed to not know my mother's address.

'I forgot,' I whisper.

'Lot of bloody good you are,' says Uncle Mick. 'Bright as everyone says you are and everything.'

The names of the different avenues, streets, roads and ways my mother's lived on over the years swirl around inside my head and I can't put my finger on a single one of them.

'Let's just forget it then,' says Uncle Mick.

On the train back to Haslemere, I try to stop staring at Aunty Wendy's huge belly – Nan's told me it's rude to stare at anyone, ever. I focus instead on the scene through the train window; the trees' spiky silhouettes.

A question bubbles up.

'Why didn't my mum want to keep me for herself when I was born?'

'I've no idea, love,' says Aunty Wendy.

'What about my dad?' I say and my own voice surprises me; it comes out almost as a scream.

'Your dad's sittin' right here,' says Uncle Mick, pointing at his own chest.

But his words only remind me that I've got a real dad out there, probably still alive, who doesn't care enough to come and find me. And Uncle Mick's got a little girl or little boy of his own on the way.

We've managed to miss the last train from Haslemere back to Fernmere and because Nanny's the only one in the family who can drive, we must beg her to come and fetch us. I hear Nanny's annoyed voice filling the phone box.

'I'll be there in three quarters of an hour,' she snaps.

'How on earth can it take you that long? It's only eight miles,' says Aunty Wendy.

'I'm not ready, am I? It's not like I sit around just waiting for your phone calls, Wendy. I have to go and put my face on.'

Nanny turns up an hour later, with her lips painted as red as a clown's. She revs the car and speeds ahead even before Uncle Mick's closed the car door.

'You all right, Mum?' says Aunty Wendy. 'You're driving like the blazes.'

'No, I am not all right,' says Nanny. 'I have been accused of murdering Gramps.'

'You what, Mum?' Aunty Wendy's neck grows pink and inflamed.

Uncle Mick, sitting next to me in the back seat, elbows me in the side, chuckles to himself and twirls his finger against the side of his forehead, showing me he thinks Nanny is mental.

Uncle Mick has said Nanny's got a disease called Obsessive-Compulsive Disorder which is why she washes her hands about a hundred times a day. 'She wants fucking locking up, the old girl,' he whispers in my ear now.

He wouldn't dare say that to Nanny's face. Nanny might be slightly mental but I reckon Uncle Mick's slightly scared of her all the same. He never even swears in front of her.

'If you want to know what I'm talking about,' says Nanny, almost crossing a red light. 'Ask Agnes.'

But before any of us has a chance to ask Agnes, Agnes packs her suitcase and runs away from home.

How To Levitate

IT'S A GLOOMY, STARLESS night and there are hardly any street lights where we are, which is just across the border from Fernmere, in a hamlet called Hop's Corner.

'There she is, Nanny!' I say. 'Over there!'

A few yards ahead of us is Agnes, carrying a small suitcase, wearing my rabbit fur jacket and marching fiercely along the dirt road in the dark like a little female soldier.

'Let's get her, the little bitchie!' says Nanny, slowing the car down and stalking Agnes, the way Tom stalks Jerry. 'Unlock the car door, Nin. We'll make her get in the back with you.'

'Get her, Nanny! Get her!'

It doesn't occur to me that I'm betraying Agnes. I'm so charged up on adrenalin and outrage that she's daring to leave that I do not think at all.

Agnes turns her head and her scared eyes are illuminated by Nanny's headlights. We swerve after her as she turns off the dirt road and along a winding driveway. Nanny lowers her car window and chants, 'Get in, Aggy! Get in!'

At the end of the driveway, there's a large house in front of which Nanny screeches to a halt. Approaching our car are a girl from my year at school called Sasha, Sasha's parents and Agnes's really-quite-weird friend Christine, who is Sasha's big sister. Four pairs of eyes peer at us through Nanny's car window, making me feel like a guppy in a tank.

'What do you want?' asks Christine in her slow-motion giggly voice. Agnes stands next to Christine who squeezes Agnes's arm and giggles. We all stare at Christine. She covers her mouth with her hand and looks down at the gravel.

'Can I help you, Mrs Taylor?' says Sasha's dad, reaching out to take Agnes's suitcase.

'I've come to get Agnes and stop this nonsense,' says Nanny.

'We're not making her get in the car with you,' says Sasha's dad.

'Then I'll call the damned police,' says Nanny.

'Feel free to,' he says. 'You're not Agnes's legal guardian, and she's over eighteen. She's welcome to stay here with us for as long as she likes.'

We watch Agnes disappear through the door of her new home, followed by Christine, Sasha's parents and Sasha – who waves at me and grins. When the door slams shut, there's nothing for us to do but drive away.

More than a quarter of a century later, I sit in this driveway once again, with Agnes and Agnes's new husband, Wachuku. Agnes is giving Wachuku a guided tour of her past.

'I was so sad when you went into that house and shut the door,' I tell Agnes. 'I couldn't bear it that you were leaving me.'

'Precious, really?' Agnes says, genuinely shocked. 'I never knew. I didn't think you felt anything, the way you just sat there egging Nanny on like Nanny's little henchman.'

'What else could I do? If I didn't do what Nanny wanted then I could have lost her as well as losing you.'

The house we're sitting in front of is smaller than we both remember it. Its door opens and a middle-aged white man emerges and peers through the window of Wachuku's car.

'Can I help you with anything?' he says, eyes roaming from Wachuku's gold tooth to my dreadlocks. He takes two or three steps backwards. In this part of West Sussex, even in 2007, our presence – three black people in a jeep blazing Notorious B.I.G. – is like a vaguely menacing question mark.

'We're looking for a Christine Baker,' Agnes says.

'The Baker family left here in the 1980s,' the man replies, incredulously.

Once it's clear Agnes is not getting in the car, that we've lost her, Nanny drives me to our favourite haunt, Lily Pond, to see if we can 'calm our nerves' by taking a look at the heron that lives among the rushes. But when we get to Lily Pond, all we can see in the moonlight are the shadows cast over the water by the reeds growing at the edges of the pond. We sit in darkness.

'You can't really blame Agnes for being a bit confused,' says Nanny. 'Things haven't been exactly easy for Agnes, thanks to your mother. Why do you think poor Else always made sure she was scarce whenever your mother turned up? The pair of them *never* saw eye to eye. It just wan't fair on her, the way your mother dragged her here from Africa, from everything she knew and loved.'

Agnes never returns to 52 West Walk. I've no idea how long she stays in Hop's Corner with the Baker family. Eventually I hear – via Sasha at school – that Aggy's gone to London.

During the months that follow, Agnes – who loves gossip the way I love Wagon Wheels – appears to still be in touch with our mother. I overhear crumbs of increasingly melodramatic adult conversations and Agnes is at the centre of them all. Agnes has supposedly been told by my mother that Nanny tipped Gramps in his wheelchair down the stairs, killing him on purpose to release herself from the burden of looking after him. How on earth my mother would claim to know this is beyond me and, anyway, Gramps died after slipping on the floor while using the loo. His fall led to a heart attack and he died in hospital.

My mother's also supposedly told Agnes she's planning to remove me permanently from Nanny's 'any day now'. But my mother regularly makes similar threats and I've learned not to believe a word of any of it.

Much of this web of intrigue and threats evaporates once Aunty Wendy's fat, pink baby girl Kelly is born. Kelly's bald except for a stripe of blond hair down the centre of her head, which makes her look a little like Uncle Mick's dad, Uncle Malcolm.

Kelly's a miracle baby for two reasons – first because Aunty Wendy wasn't even trying to get pregnant when she did, and secondly because Kelly isn't handicapped – unlike Aunty Wendy's first baby, Christian, who died soon after he was born.

Christian had an illness called Lees Disease and he died when I was about four. My memories of him revolve around a single image, a golden-haired gentle baby boy who never seemed to move.

Winter of 1980 brings a letter that instantly changes our lives. I recognise the large, spidery scrawl on the envelope at once – my mother's handwriting. Nanny reads the letter out to me over breakfast.

The letter says Mummy Elizabeth wants to talk to Nanny about my future. She's had enough of how boring and dull I am and she is finding absolutely no pleasure at all in interacting with me. Something's got to be done. So she's going to be removing me from Nanny's care in the near future and sending me back to Africa.

The enclosed cheque, for my keep, flutters onto the kitchen table. I watch Nanny fold the letter in half and slide it back into its blue envelope.

'I'm keeping this as evidence,' she says cryptically. 'There is no way I am letting that bitch take you to Africa again. I'm not having it. She's given me no choice but to go a solicitor, Anita.'

I digest the contents of my mother's letter – and I have questions, questions, questions. Excitement overlaid with dread. There's an urge rising in me to speak up, to ask my questions, but Nanny's face warns me to remain quiet. I want to know why Nanny's so sure that going to Africa is automatically bad. Uncle Mick said once that it would make him sad if I ever went there for good but that he understands that, at the end of the day, I'm an African. Why does Nanny see it all so differently then?

And what about if I went to live with Aunty Wendy and Uncle Mick instead? Would Mummy Elizabeth then let me stay in Fernmere? I'd be happy living in Aunty Wendy's house; I'd be allowed to go out and play with the other kids on the estate and I wouldn't have to keep washing my hands all the time.

It takes Nanny mere minutes to find a solicitor, making me suspect she's had one up her sleeve all along, in preparation for this moment. The solicitor's name is Mr Braithwaite, a man Nanny calls 'a hell of a chap'. We go to his office. He's dressed in a pinstriped suit and sits at a desk the colour of milk chocolate that's piled high with faded hardback books. He wears an enormous watch and his dainty wrist looks like it could snap under the weight of all that heavy metal – real gold, I think.

Nanny tells me I must put my best foot forward and we must 'present a good case' to a lot of very distinguished people who are going to be interviewing me and asking my opinions about things. There is no opportunity, it seems, for me to ask questions or to voice my fears. I am the one who will be questioned.

I prepare myself for this scrutiny by locking myself away. When not at school or asleep or eating, I try to spend as much time as I can shut inside the cupboard beneath the stairs, sitting at a makeshift desk Uncle Mick put together for me, flicking through piles of fusty library books with brittle pages. Aunty Wendy makes frequent attempts to coax me out, to get me to go out and play with my friends, but I'm stubborn and, anyway, Nanny thinks I should be allowed to spend my time alone with a stack of books if that's what I want.

I hear a voice outside my cupboard: low, conspiratorial. It's Aunty Julia, the wife of Nanny's posh-voiced son Dave. 'I'm very fond of Anita,' she says. 'But I've always thought she was a strange little girl.'

Here we go again. Another of Aunty Julia's sermons about how I should be out interacting with my peers, not spending all this time by myself.

'She's just a shy little thing,' says Nanny. 'There's nothing wrong with my Nin at all.'

Nanny always contradicts Aunty Julia because she is keen to put her in her place. According to Nanny, Aunty Julia's mum used to be Nanny's housekeeper, back in the days before Woodview, when Nanny was still middle-class.

Aunty Julia's not entirely wrong about me, I suppose. I *am* strange. Here I am, nine years old and reading books about Indian holy men and yoga, when I could be out climbing trees or roller-skating through the Woodview streets with my friends. But life inside my cupboard is so much more interesting. According to my books, the Indian holy men can literally float in the air. All it takes to float in the air is the right frame of mind, the books say.

I take notes in my exercise book, close my eyes and imagine sailing up into the sky. The books say that in order to be 'enlightened' one must avoid certain 'poisonous' foods – and that's why I've decided to give up orange squash and tomato ketchup.

When I tell Nanny this news about my new dietary requirements, she smiles and says, 'Oh really, darling? How long will that last?'

'I wouldn't have it, Mum,' Aunty Wendy says.

When I am next at Aunty Wendy's house, Uncle Mick makes a point of squirting a huge blob of ketchup onto my chips. 'Eat it,' he says.

I do not say 'no'. I just sit there in silence, meditating.

'Eat your bloody tea!' Uncle Mick picks up a ketchup-sodden chip from my plate and angles it towards my mouth.

'I can't eat it,' I say.

'What do you mean, you bloody can't?'

He soon gives up and crams the chip into his own mouth.

'This is ridiculous,' says Aunty Wendy. 'There's something wrong with you, my girl. Nanny needs to stop letting you get away with this nonsense.'

'Here comes the future Dr Williams,' says my mother, scanning me for faults and weaknesses as I walk into her parlour with Uncle Abejide, who has just picked me up from Fernmere.

There are two unfamiliar women in the parlour: a petrified-looking brown girl holding a tiny baby and a white woman with a haystack wedge of hair who introduces herself to me as Mrs Berry, Court Welfare Officer.

I sit there trembling, afraid of my mother's scrutiny. My hair is a mass of wild knots and clumps and she's bound to say something any second now.

'Even her grandmother, her father's mother, was very brilliant,' says my mother. 'She was doing her doctorate at Oxford University.'

So the paternal grandmother I've never met is a doctor then. Not a medical doctor, I learn later, but rather a PhD in English Literature. So that's why my mother wants me to become Dr Williams when I grow up. The only doctor I know is Dr Gillies, poking his little wooden sticks down people's throats and his tiny lamp up people's noses. I'm thrilled when my mother boasts about the jobs my family members hold and reels off lists of their academic achievements. It's a reminder to me that I have a lot of very clever people in my real family. Maybe one day I will take after them.

There are two new silver-framed pictures on the formerly bare walls: one is of my mother in a crocheted ivory bridal gown, towering over Uncle Abejide; the other a picture of a baby who looks like a newborn seal; all big eyes and smooth sleek skin, the baby who's now lying in the lap of a stranger opposite me, gurgling.

'Aren't you going to say hello to your brother?' my mother says.

'He's beautiful, mother. What's his name?'

'James. But we call him Chuka.'

'Are you going to keep him?'

'Of course I'm going to keep him. Be polite, Nitty. This is Chimamanda, who I brought over from Chukaro to help me with him. And this is some kind of social worker,' she jerks her thumb at Mrs Berry. 'Say hi.'

'Hi,' I say.

Chimamanda looks up and smiles shyly.

'Hallo, Anita,' says Mrs Berry. 'I'm here to see how you get on with your mother.'

What on earth? Even I, aged nine, can see that this is a complete load of crap. Of course nobody is going to act like their normal self in front of a spectator from the High Courts. Does this Mrs Berry think we're thick or what?

Mrs Berry asks my mother questions but my mother speaks to Ngozi and Uncle Abejide in Igbo rather than answering any of the questions. The only thing she says to Mrs Berry is: 'I've enrolled Anita in a local private school.' As if this information exempts her from needing to answer further questions.

'I'll need to speak to Anita briefly on her own for a minute,' says Mrs Berry.

And off we go into my mother's kitchen where Mrs Berry sits opposite me, pen poised. The questions erupt out of her and I answer her just as rapidly, without thinking clearly about what I'm saying.

'Apart from Mum,' Mrs Berry says, 'do you have contact with any other people of your own ethnicity?'

'What's ethnicity?'

'Coloured people.'

'My sister. But she ran away from us. And Eddie.'

'How often do you see Eddie?'

'I've seen him twice so far. His mother's one of my mother's friends from Africa.'

Mrs Berry scribbles something in her notepad.

'I see. Where would *you* like to live, Anita, if you could choose?'

'Do I have to say?'

I'm wearing a blue-and-white gingham sundress which Nanny spent twenty minutes ironing this morning. I rub my palms against the stiffened fabric to calm my nerves and wipe the sweat off my hands.

'I'd like to hear what you have to say, yes.'

'I'd live with my dad.'

'But your dad's not in the picture, is he?'

'Which picture?'

'You don't see much of Dad, do you? Where does Dad live?'

'I never see him. He lives in America.'

'How did you find out that he was living in America?'

'I just *know*, that's all.'

'When did you last see Dad?'

'I don't think I ever have.'

'Anita,' Mrs Berry leans forward, really peering at me. 'This might be a difficult question for you to answer, but I need to ask you whether anyone has ever touched you in a way that made you feel uncomfortable?'

I shrug my bare shoulders and shiver a little, even though it's very hot in the kitchen.

Earlier, at breakfast, Nanny said, 'if you say the wrong thing, darling, they'll send you straight to Africa and you'll get terribly ill again. And you won't have any of your friends or any of your toys.'

I'm not sure whether I'm allowed to tell this drained-looking beige-toothed lady the truth about my life so far. Have I ever felt uncomfortable? Let's put it this way, only very occasionally have I ever felt comfortable. In my life or in my body. But if I say this, if I tell the truth, I'm pretty sure I'd be letting both my mother *and* Nanny down and then what would be left?

'I've never felt uncomfortable,' I say.

The following morning, my mother says, 'I'm taking you to the hair salon. If you're going to live with me, you've got to look decent. You've got to do something with your hair.'

I'm very excited about finally having straight hair because my bushy, brittle hair is the main thing that makes me so ugly. I don't want to be a pube-head anymore: I want hair that swings and shines and reaches my shoulders.

Gloria's Hair Salon and Braiding Centre smells disappointingly of disinfectant and rotten eggs. While my mother watches, looking bored and impatient, Gloria smoothes a stinking yellow cream into my head and combs my hair with a fine-tooth comb. I monitor her progress in the huge mirror in front of me. As my hair is combed, it stretches like plasticine until finally it is hanging down flat, smearing the rotten-egg creamy substance all over my neck and cheeks.

Then comes the heat. Fire ants crawling all over my scalp, and burrowing into the flesh beneath. The nape of my neck and the flesh at my temples and the tips of my ears are all ablaze and I scream and I try to leap out of the big spongy chair. The towel around my shoulders slides to the floor. My mother tells me to shut up and to stop embarrassing her and when I won't stop squirming and wincing she grips my arm hard and tells me to sit still.

'I think it must have taken by now,' says Gloria. 'Even on *her* hair.'

The warm water stings my raw scalp as the cream is rinsed out and my hair is washed with a shampoo that's bubblegum-pink but smells of apples. As clear water drips down my face, I look in the mirror. I see my mother's approving eyes reflected back at me. The true nature of my hair has been rinsed away down the plughole. Every coil and kink that once lived and thrived on my head has vanished. My tough frizz has transformed into a series of limp, straight, long-ish strands hanging wanly from my cooked scalp like over-boiled spaghetti. I am beautiful.

I get back to my mother's house, straight-haired and in love with myself, reeking of the chemicals Gloria used in her salon, tossing my head like an agitated pony. Uncle Abejide, says, 'You did your hair, Nitty!' He hands my baby brother to me.

The doorbell rings. It's Mrs Berry. My mother reluctantly lets her in.

'Hi, Mrs Berry,' I say, smoothing my new flat paper-thin hair back with my hand.

'How was your visit to the hairdresser's?' she asks, beaming. 'Don't you look beautiful?'

'How did you know I was going there?'

'A little birdy told me. How are you getting on with your little brother?'

'Do you like my hair, Nanny?'

'I'm not sure yet whether it suits you,' Nanny says.

I'm in the bath. Nanny swishes my pink flannel over my torso, lathers up a bar of Pears soap and rubs it into my wet skin. Her wrinkled fingers dance across my slippery skin like a moth's wings.

'I bet you haven't had a good wash since you went up to your mother's,' says Nanny.

I lose myself in the pattern on the pink-and-white tiles above the tub.

'Did she remember to help you clean behind your ears this time?' says Nanny, squeezing soapy water over my shoulders.

I shake my head.

'What was it like then? Up at your mother's house in London?' says Nanny.

I select the details I think Nanny will find most rewarding.

'My brother hardly ever cries,' I say. 'He's beautiful. And my mother, well she's got this weird stuff like string in her bathroom. Called dental floss. And she told me to use it on my teeth. She said that if I didn't start using it, my teeth will eventually drop out.'

'Ooh yes?' says Nanny.

Nanny's pretending to be interested but I suspect she has no real interest in hearing about tooth care. Her teeth dropped out when she was pregnant with Aunty Wendy. She chews with her gums now and hasn't had to use a toothbrush in thirty or more years.

'And my mother was in bed most of the time with her bedroom door shut and I kept hearing giggling coming out of her room. Do you like my new hair or not, Nanny?' I ask again.

'I think I prefer it when it's in those little tails, Nin,' says Nanny staring at my squeaky-clean face. 'Like dear little Topsy.'

I check out *Uncle Tom's Cabin* from Fernmere library. Nanny rang the librarian up and ordered it specially, so I could read it and love it as she loves it. I sit in my cupboard, flicking through the book, thrilled at the prospect of finally reading about this character Nanny's always insisted is 'the living spit' of me.

I whizz through chapters until I arrive at a page announcing the arrival of Topsy. Tracing the words with my finger, I drink in the author's description of Topsy. And then I stumble upon a line that reads, 'grinning like an ugly black doll', and I freeze.

I hold my breath and force myself to continue reading.

She was quite black. Her round, shining eyes glittered like glass beads. Her woolly hair was plaited into little tails which stuck out in all directions. Her clothes were dirty and ragged. Miss Ophelia thought she had never seen such a dreadful little girl in all her life.

I close the book and sit staring at the blank wall in front of me, my very worst fears about myself confirmed. So, this is how the grown-ups and the other kids see me. This is what people really think of me.

I wonder – do the social workers, the judge and the court welfare officers see me as an 'ugly black doll' as well? These social workers and court welfare officers have to write reports about me and submit them to the Family Court. It seems an enormous lot of bother to go to for a dreadful little girl. Seems even more of a waste of time when I get interviewed by the headmaster at the primary school, who sends a statement about me to the court. And my GP, Dr Gillies, sends a letter about me to the court as well.

Nanny seems excited by the action. The lawyer Mr Braithwaite gets hold of all the statements submitted and lets Nanny read them and Nanny paraphrases them to me.

'Dr Gillies has done us proud,' she says. 'I wouldn't have expected it from the miserable bugger.'

Nasal-voiced Dr Gillies has written: 'It would be psychologically very unsettling for Anita to return to the different culture of Nigeria. Anita is fully adapted to our way of life.'

But Mrs Berry, Nanny says, she's let us down. Mrs Berry's declared that although I might feel English now, I will reach a point in life where it is made very clear to me that I am not actually English at all. Like that's not damaging enough, she has also reported that I had a withdrawn and 'shut-in' look when she interviewed me. She feels I should perhaps be referred to a child psychiatrist.

Nanny says the officials are now looking into sending me to Great Ormond Street, as a residential patient for two weeks, to be assessed and interviewed by 'a leading child psychiatrist' called Dr Seaton.

'What does being assessed mean, Nanny?'

'The doctors and nurses watch you and get you to open up to them,' Nanny says.

'How do they open you up?'

'By talking to you gently, I'd imagine. I'm sure they've got all sorts of wonderful facilities up there.'

I ask question after question about Great Ormond Street and Nanny says it's a hospital that has a good reputation for helping sick little children but that it's not really a place I should go to, because there is absolutely nothing wrong with me. I am as right as rain.

I disagree. Great Almond Street, as I call it, sounds magical and I am determined to go there. Nanny tells me it's located somewhere in central London. I visualise a road made of yellow bricks leading to a lilac-coloured castle-like hospital. Inside are nurses in powder-blue uniforms, leading the children, all of us black, out to paddocks where we feed apples to ponies, a pony for every child. The nurses will feed us ice cream, speak to us tenderly, and cajole us into talking about what's troubling us.

I am a kettle so choked up with stagnant water that I can't even come to the boil and release steam. Great Almond Street, as I imagine it, is the one place in the world where the pressure will be taken off me, where I can tell the truth without suffering potentially terrifying repercussions. I want to tell someone how I feel.

If I'm to ever get all of this off my chest, I must just find my way to Dr Seaton and curl up in his hospital, sipping cocoa, and begin to talk. I can already almost feel the sweet relief that will wash over me when I finally let it all out.

'*Can* I go, Nanny?'

Nanny looks suspicious. 'I don't know whether it's a good idea or not, darling. You'd have to be away from your Nanny for two weeks. You'd have to live there. Let's wait and see what the authorities say.'

*　　*　　*

One afternoon, Aunty Wendy drops me home from school and a bald man is waiting for me in Nanny's sitting room. He's wearing wire-rimmed spectacles and sniffing as though he's coming down with a cold – or maybe it's the strong smell of Ajax in the house that's irritating his nostrils.

'I'm Mr Parsons,' he says. 'I'm with West Sussex Social Services and I'm your social worker.'

I'm not surprised when this Mr Parsons starts up with the probing questions but every time I answer one, Nanny opens her mouth as if to speak or complain but instead just rubs her hands together and stares hard at us both.

'What do you enjoy doing?' Mr Parsons says with a smile that doesn't quite reach his eyes.

'Um, reading books and comics. Watching films.'

'What kinds of films do you enjoy?'

He really doesn't sound very interested: I wonder why he wants to know.

'Westerns,' I mumble. 'And I like the *Texas Chainsaw Massacre* and *Death Race 2000*.'

'And writing stories,' says Nanny. 'She'd sit up in her room on her own writing stories until the cows came home if I let her.'

'What else do you like doing, Anita? Do you enjoy playing with your friends?'

'Not really,' I say.

'She hasn't got all that many friends around here,' says Nanny. 'There are some pretty unsavoury families on the estate so I make sure she keeps herself to herself. She had a poem she wrote printed in a comic the other day, didn't you Nin,' Nanny continues. 'I was ever so proud of her.'

Mr Parsons seems to be getting a bit fed up with Nanny. He ignores her interruptions. 'Now tell me, Anita,' he says. 'What does being an African girl mean to you?'

'It means people call me names.'

'Do you see yourself as English?'
'Yep.'

I wait, peering through the foliage. I'm not supposed to stand out in the open, on the common, but rather to scrunch myself into the actual bushes, where I'll be less conspicuous.

Nanny has helped form a search party in the town, to look for me. The search party's already phoned up Mr Franklin, my headmaster and had him open up the school grounds to check I'm not hiding in there. They've sat down with the sergeant at Fernmere Police Station to give him my photograph and description.

I don't understand the point of this game of hiding alone in the woods with nothing to do. But if I show my face I will make Nanny look bad. And then what? What if my real mother doesn't really want me back? What would happen to me then? Would Great Almond Street still take me if nobody was fighting over me anymore in court?

It started, as so many weird things do, with a phone call from my mother. I heard her screeching echo through the receiver, 'You are a violent woman and if you want violence you will get it! When my brother-in-law and my husband come down to get Anita, I assure you you will never see her again.'

And so Nanny told me to run away as soon as Uncle Abejide arrived to pick me up. I was to run as fast as I could up the common and wait in the woods for further instruction. That way, Nanny said, Uncle Abejide would get annoyed and drive off to London without me and the courts would 'see' that I hated my mother and my stepfather and that I wanted to stay in Fernmere for ever.

As soon as Uncle Abejide approached our open front door, I shot through the door, trembling, ran round the bend and off the estate. I didn't stop running until I reached the road leading to the common. The last I saw of Uncle Abejide was his white shoes as he stepped out of his blue BMW. Weeks later, in a meeting with social workers, he says, 'I knew they'd pull a stunt like this.'

Nanny's beautiful sing-song voice rings out into the foliage.

'Nin! Neety! Are you in there dear?'

I am astonished. I'd thought Nanny would send a neighbour to call me out of the bushes. For Nanny to be walking in the woods, with her asthma and her arthritis, willing to risk rips in her stockings, mud in her high-heeled shoes, this must be an extremely important occasion.

'You can come out now, darling,' she whispers. 'Your mother's husband has gone.'

The following day my mother keeps ringing us up. Nanny answers, listens, scowls and replaces the receiver. 'Your mother's just threatened to send a hitman down here to kill me and Wendy,' she says.

The phone rings again and I answer it. It's my mother again. 'What do you think you are doing,' my mother hisses. 'How can you do this to me? I'm your *mother*! What was all this pretend-running-away nonsense?'

I see myself standing in the bushes the day before. Bored, afraid, guilty. I wish I'd had the courage then to set fire to the leaves so that I'd go up in flames.

Nanny is gesturing and mouthing instructions.

'WHY?' screams my mother.

'Nanny's told me I've got to put the phone down,' I say, replacing the receiver.

Nanny sends me round to Wendy's so that Wendy can come round and answer the phone should my mother ring again.

The case rages on, taking custody of all our lives. The first hearing is in Sussex but the case gets transferred to the High Courts in London. Every day, Nanny buttons up her new mac, swipes lipstick across her mouth and leaves with Aunty Wendy for London. Nanny's posh son Dave drives down from Guildford and picks them up each morning in his fast car. The first day they go to court, Nanny chuckles, 'I haven't been to London since 1956.'

Nanny fills me in on each day's events once she's back home. It is as though she's reading articles from the *Daily Mirror* aloud. 'Your mother screamed at the judge in court this morning,' she tells me, gleefully. 'She gave her barrister the sack right there and then in front of everybody.'

'Your mother wouldn't stop screaming abuse at people in the courtroom'.

'Your mother was wearing a suit that must have cost a thousand pounds.'

'Your mother's pregnant again.'

'The paramedics had to be called to the court because it looked like your mother was about to miscarry her baby.'

'Your mother called me a devil in disguise.'

'Your mother attacked me in the court today and had to be hauled off by one of the ushers.'

I let these words and stories wash over me, feeling distanced from both the subject of these tales and their bearer. I begin to regard these adults I once yearned for – Nanny and my mother – as characters, totally removed from me. I write stories about them in my exercise book, while sitting in the cupboard. In my stories, Nanny and my mother beat each other to death and I am left alone to live happily ever after.

One night, trying to iron the trepidation and excitement out of my voice, I ask, 'When am I going up to Great Almond Street, Nanny?'

'You're not, darling. You don't have to go! That Mr Parsons has really come through for us and he's said you don't strike him as the sort of child who *needs* to see a psychiatrist at all. He thinks you're well adjusted and very happy here with your old Nanny!'

Nanny reads me a portion of Mr Parsons' report:

Anita's command of the English language is very good. Her attachment to the British way of life is evident. Mrs Taylor has devoted more time than most would have done to this coloured child.

My mother's cheques have stopped coming. She wrote to Nanny about it, explaining that there was no way she was going to pay a manipulative evil devil to steal her very own child right from under her nose. To make ends meet, Nanny takes in an extra foster kid – Jemima, the five-year-old daughter of a Ugandan doctor who's studying in London.

Jemima moves into my pink bedroom, plays with my dolls and leafs through my books. I'm moved into Nanny's bedroom. I must now knock first if I want to enter my own room. One night, I slip out of Nanny's bed and into my bedroom and stand there looking at Jemima. As I watch her chest rise and fall and her limbs flail and twist as she sleeps, I feel myself shrinking. I now understand that I am replaceable. There is very little point to me.

In the end, Jemima doesn't stay very long. She won't cooperate with Nanny in the bathroom. Instead of using the loo, she wets my bed. At night, she creeps downstairs, poos on our kitchen floor and hides her turds underneath Nanny's red-and-white pouffe. As soon as Jemima's dad's finishes his studies, we send her back. I return to my own bedroom.

One afternoon, Uncle Mick hands me a photograph of a golden-beige, round-faced baby with spiky black hair.

'This is him,' he says. 'He's all right, ain't he?'

Uncle Mick and Aunty Wendy have been sneaking off to Brighton at the weekends. Now that they have Kelly, they're applying to adopt a second baby of their own so Kelly won't be an only child. The baby boy is Indian. In Brighton, they're taking lessons with social workers to learn how to care for an Indian baby.

'He's lovely,' I say when I see the photograph. 'I love him.'

'How can you love him when you ain't even met him yet?' says Uncle Mick. 'We don't know yet whether the adoption people are gonna approve us.'

'What's his name?' I say.

'The old dear wants to call him Andrew if we get him. Says that was her old man's middle name.'

I look at the photo of this Andrew for a long time. He has a beautiful innocence to him I've never seen in my own baby photos.

'What's wrong with *me* then? Why don't you just adopt me? If you want another child of your own, I mean?'

'We tried to adopt you, didn't we?' says Uncle Mick. 'When you was tiny. Me and Wendy talked about how much we'd like to adopt you. But the old girl, the bleedin' Queen Mother, she wasn't having any of it. She wouldn't let us do it, would she? So we never had the chance.'

Fragility

IT IS NOT LONG before Nanny has a brainwave. She says that since I enjoy writing so much, I must write a letter to the judge, telling him who I'd like to win custody of me, and why. Mr Braithwaite, the solicitor, thinks this is a marvellous idea.

I, meanwhile, feel disappointed. I'd secretly begun to daydream about 'appearing' in court, being bought brand-new outfits fit to wear in front of a judge, and, most of all, stopping at Wimpy for tea each evening after the day's 'hearing' was over.

But both Mr Braithwaite and the social workers have other ideas. Nanny says they've both agreed I'm too 'fragile' to speak in court. They reference the fact I recently emptied all of Aunty Wendy's kitchen drawers onto the floor and sat amongst the debris, crying, claiming that monsters were coming to get me. And I've been caught at school, stealing a loaf of bread from one of the dinner ladies and then garbling something to the form teacher about God having given me the bread.

Mr Parsons, the social worker, feels that I'm still not in a bad enough state to be assessed by Dr Seaton, but that I'd benefit from a sedative. He writes in his report:

> Anita's general personality seems to have changed from a pleasant, happy and well-mannered child, to that of an irritable, unhappy and suspicious person.

This behaviour is not like me, the teachers say.

I'm not myself, according to Aunty Wendy.

I ask Nanny what they mean by 'fragile' and Nanny says, 'You're delicate, darling. Sensitive.'

I ask Uncle Mick why they're saying I'm 'fragile' and he says, 'It means they think you're mental.'

So Nanny takes me in to see Dr Gillies, which pleases me because it means a morning off from school. Nanny is thrilled too because there is no place she loves more than the doctor's surgery, with its hushed corridors and its antiseptic smell.

'It's her nerves, Doctor,' Nanny says.

Dr Gillies appears uninterested. Nanny is always bringing me in here. She sits by my side, boulder-like handbag in her lap, while I look at my feet and the bored doctor gets out his stethoscope and presses his icy palm against my round belly to perform another of his fruitless examinations.

Last week we came about my eczema. And in the months preceding this one, about my tonsillitis, my urinary tract infections, my sinus infections, my constipation, my headaches, the fact my feet are flat and have no instep, my hay fever, my peculiarly shaped skeleton (my bottom seems to curve up and outwards), my mood swings, my nightmares.

'She needs tranquillisers, just for a week or so, Doctor,' says Nanny. 'The social worker's said so. The nerves are affecting her studies. The poor child can't cope with the pressure of The Case.'

'I thought the social worker said I needed sedatives, Nanny,' I whisper.

'Same thing, darling,' Nanny says as Dr Gillies scrawls something unintelligible onto his prescription pad, tears it off and virtually tosses the little sheet of paper at us.

I take one of Dr Gillies's sedative/tranquilliser pills and the nightmares begin to fade to white, giving way to gorgeous soothing daydreams filled with unicorns and fairies and gnomes, good witches and puppies. Everything in my life seems at once light and unreal, like my thoughts are suddenly wrapped in candy floss. This is surely almost as good as being at Great Almond Street.

One afternoon, I sit at Aunty Wendy's kitchen table, smiling to myself and drinking Lucozade through a straw. Nanny's dehydrated hand grips my plump wrist, bringing me back from my daydreams. There is a pad of baby-blue Basildon Bond notepaper in front of me with a new Berol pen laid across it.

'Dear Judge,' I write and I sit there biting the pen, waiting for further instruction.

Nanny stands over me, holding the edge of Aunty Wendy's table tight.

'This will determine our future, Nin,' Nanny warns, and goes on to tell me, word-for-word, what to write in the letter. The letter is a mish-mash of truth and fantasy and writing it feels like writing one of my short stories. In between whispering words, Nanny's breath comes out ragged and shallow. I can smell the stale coffee on her breath.

'I have written to tell you how I feel about this court case,' I write, in my neat, joined-up writing. 'I have lived with Nanny in Fernmere for a long time and would like to remain in Fernmere.'

Aunty Wendy turns away from her washing-up to face us. She looks sceptical.

'You're being ridiculous, Mum. A kid her age wouldn't say *remain*,' Aunty Wendy says. 'The bloody courts aren't gonna believe a nine-year-old would use big words like that.'

'Will you mind your own business, Wendy, you daft bitchie,' says Nanny. I look up at Nanny, startled. She smiles down at me gently and tells me what to write for the next paragraph. She tells me to stop holding my pen so tightly as it's making my handwriting come out spiky.

'Nanny taught me to read when I was three and four,' I write.

This much of the letter is true. Nanny says I took to reading like a duck to water and that in this regard I am like Topsy who also loved reading and 'learned her letters like magic'.

'I have many friends in Fernmere,' I continue. 'And I like my teacher Mrs Southgate and my headmaster, Mr Franklin. I go to Brownies and country dancing and can swim fifty metres because I go regularly to swimming lessons. Nanny gives me lots of love and my mother does not when I have to stay there for short periods. My favourite meal is "roast" which Nanny cooks on a Sunday.

'My mother cooks hot peppery meals that hurt my throat. I am working hard at school so that I might win a scholarship to a good school. If I went to London it would take me a long time to get used to the Nigerian way of life and it would put me off work-ing at school. I had an unpleasant two weeks with my mother in the summer holidays. Obi, my cousin, stole a bar of chocolate from a shop. My mother made no attempt to take it back. So as I know it is wrong to steal, I had to. I have written this letter on my own and only me and you will see it. Yours sincerely, Anita Williams.'

My letter is sent in to the judge as evidence that I love my life in Fernmere. A photograph of me dressed up as Miss Biafra, grim-acing at the camera with a vivid nylon scarf tied mammy-style around my head, is presented to the court as evidence that I am in touch with my 'cultural background'.

But the judge is unimpressed. He says a child my age would not use such long words, that the entire tone of the letter suggests it was written by somebody other than me.

Nanny has a stack of paperwork from the judge crammed into her handbag and she starts crying as she tells me what it says. The judge has said that despite me being 'anglicised', I am still a coloured girl and that it seems best that I am re-introduced to the

African way of life and sent back to my 'perfectly good natural mother'.

But despite sort-of winning the case, my mother suddenly loses interest and stops turning up for the hearings. When the social workers and official solicitors ring her up she does not answer the phone. They write letters to her and the letters arrive back with 'return to sender' scrawled across the envelopes.

Years later, when I obtain the court files and social workers' notes from this period, I read reports claiming my mother's interest in the proceedings, and in me, waned quite suddenly in 1981. The files say my mother claimed she had no time to see me because she was travelling overseas a lot for work. She had one son and another on the way. She didn't have enough money or time to travel to Fernmere to collect me for visits. She couldn't afford the cost of long-distance phone calls from London to Fernmere.

My mother has a different story. She says she was treated in a racist, biased way. And that she felt 'put off' after reading an affidavit submitted to the court by Mr Parsons, the social worker, a man who'd written lengthy reports about my mother despite never having met her or spoken to her. Mr Parsons had submitted the following statement to the court:

> This is not an easy matter since cultural background is an important feature here and the mother's attitude towards the children is common enough amongst the tribal customs of which she is influenced. In Nigeria and many other African states most children are 'farmed out' amongst the tribe and are treated as 'possessions' and therefore Anita's mother is doing no more than her cultural background would demand. However, it would have been hoped that the completely different culture of the host country would have influenced the mother to accept a new approach to child care . . .

My heavily pregnant mother's response to the above was to collapse on the courtroom floor, 'out of anger'. She experienced severe stomach pains right there in the courtroom, she has said, and began haemorrhaging a 'scary green liquid'.

Her own mother, in Nigeria, consequently advised her that I was a revolting, treacherous child who deserved no more of my mother's time or attention. That if the stress of this 'rubbish court case' continued, my mother might die – and that no mother should be prepared to die for an undeserving child.

Neither Nanny nor my mother have custody of me now: I am a Ward of Court. Until I turn eighteen, the court has to make all the major decisions about me. The court says that for now, at least, I must remain with Nanny.

Aunty Wendy and Uncle Mick throw me a party in the newly built hut, on the marshy field that marks the edge of Woodview estate. It's to commemorate winning the case and to celebrate my eleventh birthday. Nanny would have come but her nerves are playing up, so she's at home in front of the TV.

Uncle Mick's bought me a strawberry gateau with eleven pink candles in the middle. Nanny's made a blancmange in the shape of a rabbit, nestled in a bed of bright green jelly which is supposed to look like grass. Aunty Wendy stands proudly in charge of a mop bucket filled with fruit punch that's swimming with slices of orange and chunks of pineapple.

Our DJ, Uncle Mick, puts on Dexy's Midnight Runner's single, 'Come On Eileen', and everyone starts dancing, even the boys. It's rare for a girl to have so many boys at her birthday party, but it's not because I'm well liked because I'm not, particularly.

I managed to get them here by going up to the coolest boy in school, Tom, and handing him an invitation. I did this because the last time I saw my mother, she said something to me about bold people getting everything in life that they dream of. Tom – who has taken Eddie's place in my heart – considered my invitation for a full week and came up to me on the playground and said, 'All right. I'll come.' After that, the other boys in my year begged for invitations.

'Come On Eileen' slows right down and starts to build again in tempo and Uncle Mick clamps his hands over the headphones on his head. He is jerking his hips back and forth in tune with the beat. My mother walks in just as it reaches a crescendo.

My mother's sudden arrival shocks and thrills me. She merely nods at me and ignores Aunty Wendy. Dressed in red and sparkling with gold jewellery, she plunges into the party and immediately announces that she will conduct a dancing contest. She will give the best dancer among us a twenty-pound note.

My mother marches across the rough floorboards to Uncle Mick and whispers a greeting to him, making me choke a little on my fruit punch.

It's sad Nanny's not here to see this. Nanny's been saying my mother's not welcome at my party since she hasn't contributed a penny towards the cost of it; I'd love to see Nanny saying this to my mother's face.

Uncle Mick puts Dexy's Midnight Runners back on. My friends begin dancing furiously, for all they're worth, forming a circle and nudging me – the girl with the rich, glamorous mother – into the centre of this circle. I feel bold and limitless, perhaps because Mother's attitude is contagious or perhaps because her turning up to my party after all makes me feel so special.

I close my eyes and dance, giving my body over to the beat the way a tree surrenders to the wind. I dance until I feel droplets of sweat swimming from my hairline down the sides of my face, spinning and swaying through 'Come On Eileen' and 'Dancing Queen' and 'The Lion Sleeps Tonight'.

When I open my eyes and finally stop dancing, my mother is next to me and I dare to look directly up into her amused eyes. I hold my breath and wait for her to hand me the twenty-pound note. She runs a gentle hand through my hair. 'I see the straightener didn't last,' she says. 'Your hair looks disgusting.' And she walks up to my best friend Tara and slips a twenty-pound note into the waistband of Tara's skirt.

Before she leaves, I say to my mother, 'Thank you for coming to my birthday, Mummy.'

'I wanted to wish you a happy birthday, Precious,' my mother says. Her voice is loaded with bitterness as she adds, 'I wanted to tell you that I've had another son, Chika. He nearly died before he was even born, because of you.'

After a sweat-inducing silence, I say, 'What's Chika like, Mummy?'

'My son is beautiful,' she says fiercely.

I flinch when she says 'my son', wondering why she doesn't say 'your brother'.

When Chika's lying in his mother's arms, he must not know that I exist or that she's my mother too.

'Any news of Agnes?' my mother says.

The last we heard Agnes was doing something called 'sleeping rough'. I say nothing. I want my mother to hold me, the way she must hold her new son.

'Well,' she says. 'I wanted to tell you that, after this, I'm washing my hands of you. I can't believe you chose that woman over me.'

She rubs her hands together briskly, and she walks away, across the field, her high heels stabbing the marshy soil.

BOOK THREE

How simple a thing it seems to me that to know ourselves as we are, we must know our mothers' names.

Alice Walker, *In Search of Our Mothers' Gardens*

Who I Am

I'M SITTING ON A scarred wooden bench, with condom wrappers and broken Diamond White bottles at my feet. Chewing gum's stuck to the graffiti'd walls around me. An obscured, faded bus timetable, dotted with fag burns, advertises the sluggish, infrequent passage of buses to and from Haslemere, Pompey, Chichester and Bognor.

Sitting next to me: Tom. Just about the coolest, best-looking boy in my year at school. Unbelievably, his arm is draped around me. I pretend, in this delicious second, that he fancies me. Even though I know better. Truth is, when the two of us hang out like this, Tom talks non-stop about other girls – the girls he fancies. White girls. Blond girls. And I just listen. Or sometimes I give him advice about his love life. Like I know anything about romance.

A car cruises the perimeter of the bus station; a white car that's as rusty and insubstantial-looking as an ancient Diet Coke can. It inches towards us and its windows slide down on the passenger side. Wendy leans out. 'What do you think you're doing, you idle little devil?' she yells.

'Can't I stay?' I look at Tom who's staring at Wendy.

'We've been driving all over the town looking for you,' she screams. 'What the hell do you think you're doing in this disgusting bus shelter? You're coming grocery shopping with us, my girl. It doesn't hurt you to give Nanny a hand.'

'I'll see you later, Tom, yeah?' I whisper, inching apathetically towards Nanny's car.

Nanny turns in her seat and narrows her crinkle-rimmed eyes at me. She purses her matt-scarlet lips. And then she revs the engine.

'Mick said he saw you with that little waste-of-space Debbie earlier,' says Wendy.

'So?'

'My Mick said you refused to tell him where you were off to. God I don't know how you can go around with that Debbie. Dunno what germs you might pick up from being around her.'

'Well I'm not having sex with her am I?'

'Will you shut up, for Pete's sake, you insolent little slut! This is the second week in a row you've tried to skive off coming shopping. I've got my spies. I know what you get up to.'

I may be insolent but I'm definitely not a slut. In theory I could have become one. I value my body so little that I'd probably let absolutely anyone do absolutely anything to it. But I don't put it about, I don't get around. Because the intense disgust I feel at the very thought of sex overrides *everything*. And so I am laughably chaste. Never snogged a boy, never gone on a date.

Not that anybody's queueing up to get off with me anyway. The only guys who find me at all pretty are not my peers but rather the grown men who occasionally sidle up to me at the bus station or at my part-time waitressing job, calling me a 'sexy little jungle bunny'. Telling me, 'You ain't half exotic.'

'You know what they say,' says Wendy. 'Hang around with dogs and you'll wake up with fleas.'

'You're so fucking sad,' I hiss.

'*What* did you say?'

'Forget it.'

'That was that Tom you were with, wasn't it? What were you doing with him then? Slow down, Mum.' Wendy pokes her finger through the open car window as we crawl up Chichester Road. 'That's where that Tom lives, isn't it?'

Craning her neck and peering through the car window, Wendy takes in the details; the large detached house set back from the main road, the unblemished white Mercedes parked in front, the beautifully tended flower beds. Wendy turns to look at me, a curious smile on her face. 'What are you doing knocking about with someone like him then?' she says.

'What's it got to do with you who I go round with?'

'You don't half have an attitude, my girl,' says Wendy. 'You don't half think highly of yourself. I love you and I always will, but I don't know who you think you are.'

Who I am is a thoroughly English girl. The colour of my skin doesn't mean a thing. I'm as white as the next person. *Inside.* I know nothing about Africa. I care nothing about Africa. And everyone in Fernmere is so used to me now, so friendly with me, that they see me as one of their own. This is the fantasy, Nanny's fantasy, of how my life is.

Then there's my reality. Someone's spray-painted a message for me across one of the garage doors on Woodview. ANITA GO HOME, YOU WOG. The message was probably left by the same National Front boys who sometimes follow me home from school, throwing stones at me, hissing, 'What you got to say for yourself then, *Sambo*?'

My social worker, Barbara, has been to the police station to report the 'racialist abuse' but the cops can't do anything unless one of the stones thrown at me actually hits me. Or unless one of the NF boys himself hits me.

Life would be a lot easier for me if I didn't act so stuck-up, Barbara says. Or if I didn't keep 'going on all the time about being black', Wendy says. Barbara disagrees with Wendy and says my 'ethnicity' can't be ignored. Barbara talks about it – my colour – like it's a disease and over the years has advised me that I need to accept it, deal with it, overcome it, live with it, get to grips with it, adapt to it and stop being so sensitive about it.

Barbara comes to visit Nanny and me at six-monthly intervals, to talk to me about my 'situation', and to interview us both so that she can draw up an evaluation report that she shares with the other senior social workers. According to her latest evaluation report, the situation looks like this:

> *Mrs Taylor needs to examine her own motivation for fostering Anita and to learn to 'let go' and allow her to develop her own identity. Mrs Taylor is not always able to act clearly in Anita's best interests, owing to her own emotional need for the child. She lacks understanding of the need for Anita to be aware of and to accept her own cultural background.*

Nanny reads this report and calls it 'poppycock'.

I don't care what the grown-ups say: I don't feel like blending in any more. I've no inclination to continue apologising for the colour of my skin. I want to be allowed to be me. But then, can I really be me when I am not a hundred per cent sure who *me* is yet?

At school, I belong to every social subset going. I am an outcast in outdated Marks and Spencer get-up and at the same time I hang out with the clever, the popular and the trendily dressed kids. I'm a teacher's pet, at times, but when I feel like it, I transform into the lippy thorn in the teachers' sides – I become the kid who sits at the back of the classroom, lobbing scrunched-up paper at the teachers' backs as they write on the blackboard.

I'm a great admirer of the kids who smoke puff and of those who get arrested and the ones who get expelled. I worship the boys who carry flick knives in their rucksacks and the girls who give blow jobs in the bus shelter to boys they're not even going out with. But me, I just teeter on the precipice of delinquency; I never fully make the leap. Something – the risk of disappointing Nanny? My pride? – prevents me diving in.

I've got ambition. I want to escape to London and get my own flat and write stories for magazines and find a posse of black friends who – hopefully – will teach me how to stop being a laughing stock among other blacks.

Other black people mesmerise me but I only see them on TV – sprinting, doing the long jump, singing, dancing, rioting, stealing cars and sometimes stabbing or shooting at one another.

Last time I saw young black people – in real life and en masse – was when I went on a school trip up to the National History Museum. There they were: a crew of black kids in Adidas trainers, standing outside the museum chatting, posing, larger than life. Unmistakeably Londoners because of their sharp accents, their swagger. I stood there, in my navy school skirt and my lace-up Clarks shoes, staring at them like they were images on a cinema screen, sucking in the sweetness of every detail. One of the crew, a girl with thin, tight cornrows, stared right back at me, and yelled, 'Picky head!' and her mates looked me over quickly and erupted into rounds of chainsaw-like laughter.

At Fernmere Grammar, which is in fact the local comprehensive, there are only two other black kids – one of them's fostered over in Petworth, the other one lives at a nearby childrens' home. Being Fernmere blacks they're not what you'd call authentic. Like me, they're well versed in playing the 'please accept me' game; a game that's about subtly hating yourself and silently apologising all the time. And if you don't play the game, white people will write you off as threatening. The key to surviving in Fernmere, when you're black, is making whites believe that deep down you wish you were white yourself.

I'm growing up. I'm absolutely full of myself, I'm told, which I think is a good thing. I've always had opinions. But now, for reasons I think have to do with me recently devouring *Their Eyes Were Watching God*, I'm speaking up. Sometimes.

Wendy and Nanny say I'm growing out of control; that I'm growing more and more unbearable every day. The two of them bring out baby pictures of me and say, 'Wish you were still like that, eh?' holding them up to me as though holding garlic up in the face of a vampire.

The summer I turn sixteen we go to Hayling Island where we rent a beach-front house. Me, Nanny, Wendy, Mick, Kelly and Andrew. I buy a black hat with a wide brim from Tammy Girl and I wear it nearly every day of the holiday. I even wear it when I plunge into the choppy sea.

'I don't know how you can go about like that in that hat. It's like you *want* to look different from everyone else,' Wendy says. 'Don't you wanna just fit in? We've done everything to make you blend in. I don't understand how you could do that. Wear a hat when no one else is wearing one, for no reason.'

'She's tryin' to look like that Mel and Kim,' says Mick.

On the second-to-last day of our holiday, we go on a family trip to Havant Hypermarket where I pick up a copy of a magazine it's rare to find outside of London, *Black Beauty & Hair*. I'm sitting in the passenger seat of Mick's Ford Escort, flicking through the magazine, running my eyes over the glossy lips and glossy hair-dos.

'Black beauty and bloody hair. What's all that then?' says Mick, trying to peek at the shiny pages. 'Why're you tryin' to be something you're not, then?'

Mick's the one who actually paid for the magazine after Wendy coaxed him into treating me. So why's he complaining?

'I'll do what I want,' I say. 'I'll wear what I want.'

'You're getting ever so arrogant, Neet,' says Wendy. 'Just like your mother.'

'Good.'

On our final afternoon at Hayling Island, a white woman perched not far from us on the pebbly beach asks me, 'How did you get your hair so damn curly?'

'It grows like that doesn't it, Neet?' says Wendy. 'It's not easy to look after it, poor kid. We've been all over the place trying to find the right products.'

'I love my hair actually,' I say suddenly. 'White people are allowed to like their hair just the way it is. Why shouldn't I?'

Wendy stares at me and I put my black hat back on, get up from our beach blanket and tiptoe into the sea.

Driving home from Hayling Island, Nanny and I get as far as Chichester before there is an explosion. Ever since she had to have stomach surgery when she was in her forties, Nanny's bowels have caused her problems. When she's nervous, like she is driving on the motorway today, Nanny's bowels grow irritated; to her horror and embarrassment, there are rare occasions when she can't quite make it to the toilet in time.

The diarrhoea smell lingers, even with the car windows open. Nanny sits there stoically. She doesn't make eye contact.

'I'm sorry, love,' she says.

I turn and look through the window, fighting back tears.

Nanny pats my arm.

I turn to her, and have an explosion of my own.

'I hate this,' I sob. 'It's disgusting. *You're* disgusting. I hate you.'

Nanny is silent for a long time.

'After all I've done for you, Nin,' she says, eventually. 'I've been your biggest defender. All these years.'

'I'm just sick of this,' I sob.

'And I'm sick of *you*,' says Nanny, her voice dangerously low. 'I'm sick of your little outbursts, you spiteful, ungrateful little bitch. I spent all of my savings on you, on that court case. And nothing's ever good enough for you, is it?'

'It's your fault! *You're* the one who took me away from my mother.'

'*Took you away from your mother?*' Nanny spits. '*Took* you away from your mother? Don't you go getting any delusions about *her*: that woman didn't want you, Nin. She threw you away like a piece of rubbish. She advertised you in a magazine. She never even *liked* you, Nin.'

'She's my mother! It's your fault she won't have anything to do with me!'

'There's only one person in this world who's ever been a mother to you, my girl. Here was I thinking I was doing something nice for a little girl who needed me,' says Nanny, weeping. 'And you go and throw it all in my face.'

She may not think much of my personality these days, but Nanny's confident I'll sail through my O Levels. I can't imagine why. My English teacher may well call me 'extraordinarily skilful and colourful' but the rest of my teachers have all but written me off, using phrases like 'scatty', 'in a dream-like state' and 'obviously very able but idle' in my school reports. Plus I regularly forge Nanny's signature on sick notes and bunk off school so that I can sit alone in the town library, staring into space, daydreaming, pretending to be revising.

My O Level results, when they arrive, stun everybody except Nanny and perhaps Wendy. I've passed all eight exams: I got As in English Language and in English Literature; Bs in the humanities. I can't help wondering whether the examinations board has assigned somebody else's results to my name in error.

Here's Mick, carrying his snooker cue, looming out of the darkness like an apparition, his shoulders stooped forward as he saunters across the road. He sees me loitering by the entrance to the Duck Pond, spotlit by a street lamp.

'Hark at the state of you!' he says. 'All done up like that! Where you off to then?'

I'm wearing a purple bat-wing jumper and matching eyeshadow with a pale violet rah-rah skirt and electric blue leather-look ankle boots.

'I'm not going anywhere,' I say.

'What you doin' then, little idiot? Walkin' around in the dark on your own?'

'Yeah.'

'Why?'

'Because I want to.'

'Walk down the town with me, then.'

Mick's on his way to the pub to play in a tournament. We take a shortcut around the Duck Pond, towards the centre of the town. There is silence, aside from the eerie rustle of the ducks passing through the foliage.

Mick says, 'Why are you always lookin' so miserable lately then? I heard you passed all your exams and that – what's the matter with you? Those racialist pillocks been picking on you again then at school?'

'No. I mean, yes. But it's not that', I say and I begin to cry. 'It's just that I haven't heard from my mother or Agnes for four whole years. I don't even know my own mother's address or phone number. Why doesn't anybody love me, Mick?'

'All of us love you, don't we?' says Mick. 'You knows we do.'

'Do I?'

'Course you do.'

'I really hate my life.'

'I dunno why you always seems to expect so much out of life, Neeta. I hate my bloody life as well, Neet, but there's no use keep complainin' about it.'

Precious

NANNY CALLS ON HER clever grown-up son, Uncle Dave, to take me out for a cup of tea and talk to me about my career choices. Uncle Dave has a degree, a good job and a four-bedroom, detached house. He was even a graduate student once. So he must know what he's on about.

'My English teacher's said I've got what it takes to be a reporter or an author,' I blurt out. Then I want to kick myself for seeming arrogant. Uncle Dave smiles at me fondly. He says, 'Look, love, we know you'd like to pursue something creative. But those types of jobs don't grow on trees. It can be very difficult to get your foot in the door.'

Uncle Dave talks to me about the possibility of going to college or university and then beginning as a secretary or PA within a media company. I sit there thinking 'I'm going to become a writer and nobody – not even you – can stop me.' I cock my head as if acquiescing and I silently I decide to do exactly what Uncle Dave's just said I can't do; I'll get my size seven foot in the door just like that, thanks.

After my chat with Uncle Dave I ring up the *Fernmere Observer*, ask to speak to the editor, tell her about my O Level results and offer my services as a trainee reporter. The editor's voice bubbles with amusement. She tells me I'm welcome to apply for unpaid work experience during the holidays, and she warns me that to become a journalist, I'll need A Levels 'at least'. Which is why I sign up to take three of them, at Chichester College of Technology.

*   *   *

I presume Chichester Tech will be a cross between a funfair and a university campus. That I'll hang out with new friends in an oak-panelled canteen, discussing Charles Dickens and Maya Angelou and my brand-new love, hip-hop. But this is not to be. I spot only one black student. His blue overalls and the tool-box he carries suggest he's studying Construction. I try to strike up a conversation with him and he walks straight past me, avoiding eye contact.

My A Level English class is mainly made up of local Sloanes from Chichester and Lavant. Several of them are alumni of Lavant House, the girls' boarding school where Mick's mum works as a dinner lady. They hate hip-hop and they love miserable old Morrissey. Most of them have never spoken to a black person before in their lives. Worse still, they seem to *live* to take the piss out of the few council-estate dwellers audacious enough to have enrolled for A Level English.

I make an earnest effort to blend in with the Sloanes – by immediately pretending not to live on a council estate. Poppy and Flora and Tabitha and Pippa seem neither to like nor dislike me. They watch me closely, like I'm someone who can't necessarily be trusted and I watch them just as closely. I notice how they constantly sweep back their shoulder-length manes and how they all wear the same uniform of faded Levi 501s, white T-shirts, leather penny loafers, Benetton sweaters and blue or red paisley bandanas. I wonder if it's time to throw away my rah-rah skirts.

Eventually I grow so sick of not fitting in again that I write to *Black Beat International* magazine, asking for pen pals. My letter says, 'I'm a Nigerian girl fostered by white people in a West Sussex village and I'm looking for pen pals who can give me information about my cultural background.'

As I read through what I've just written I feel for the first time a sense of rage about my history, about the unanswered questions it presents. A single, angry word percolates then erupts up into my irritated mind: *Why?*

Why was it deemed OK for this to become my story? Why does it make the news when a little white girl is molested or beaten or neglected, when in my case it didn't even make anybody raise an eyebrow or demand an investigation? And why, if I had to be fostered at all, did it have to happen in such a makeshift way and in all-white West Sussex?

My letter's published in *Black Beat International* and I receive more than fifty replies, including a parcel from Lagos containing a voluminous scarlet and gold wax-print kaftan.

A fifty-year-old man from Ghana writes, 'I want you to know Anita Williams that your people here in Africa love you and I really feel for you after reading your wonderful letter in a magazine. I am sure your parents love you too and are longing for your touch.'

I soon have thirty pen pals, forming a link to something that feels very far away from me and yet essential to my survival: a black community.

Mick finds a plastic and wood-veneer record player in the Lost & Found cupboard at the Grange, the leisure centre where he works as caretaker. He presents it to me as a gift, to cheer me up. I begin to spend evenings hiding from Nanny, shut inside my bedroom, dancing around to the tinny sounds of my record player, listening to Stetsasonic and Masta Ace, the Cookie Crew and the Wee Papa Girls. Hip-hop captures my imagination and delights and nourishes me in a way no other medium ever has, or could, or ever will. Hip-hop burns away my apathy, to an extent. And it's my own discovery. Discovered via reading *Black Beat International*, the magazine no one else in Fernmere reads, the one the newsagent orders especially for me.

I picture them – black guys and black girls from the New York projects, standing on street corners, rattling off riveting rhymes, just like that. MC Shan. Kurtis Blow. LL Cool J. Roxanne Shante. Thrusting themselves into verbal duels, street-battles, the likes of which haven't been seen or heard since Shakespeare. Like Mercutio battling Tybalt. And these black men and women, these street poets, they don't even need to write their shit down. It's like their stories, words and verses are tattooed into their consciousness.

I sleep wearing headphones and spend all of my wages from my part-time waitressing job at Our Price, foregoing new clothes to own the latest US import LPs.

One night, just before Christmas, the Sloanes surprise me by asking me to hang out with them at the Hole In The Wall pub. I'm flattered, but there's a problem: the last bus home to Fernmere leaves Chichester at 8.30 p.m. and since the journey's twelve miles, it's too far to walk. But then Mick, who's recently learned to drive, says, 'Go on, go out with your mates. I don't mind drivin' in and picking you up.'

And so I finally have a social life. The Sloanes still know nothing about hip-hop but it's someone to go around with, isn't it? It's something to do. And so, every Thursday or Friday night I knock back pint after pint of cider with the Sloanes in the Hole In The Wall, then I ring Mick, who drives me home to Nanny, who'll hiss, 'Don't think I can't smell the alcohol on your breath you sneaky little bitchie.'

One evening Poppy asks, 'Who's that, like, middle-aged white guy who picked you up the other night in a blue car?'

I'm certainly not about to reveal to these Sloanes that I'm a foster-kid who lives on a council estate.

'He's, like, my uncle,' I say. 'His name's Mick.'

The Sloanes immediately christen him 'Cruising Capri Mick' – even though my Mick drives a Ford Escort, not a Ford Capri. They say Mick reminds them of the stereotypical boy-racer who has fluffy dice dangling in front of his car windscreen and Go Faster stripes running down the sides of his car.

I try to see Mick through their eyes: his nicotine-yellowed fingers, the way he sits in his battered Ford Escort smoking rollies and smiling mysteriously to himself through his car window. I laugh along with them but secretly I despise them for mocking him. I love Cruising Capri Mick who's more like a father to me every day. He's interested in my life and he's amused by my posh new friends.

'Who was that stuck-up little blonde then?' he says one evening. 'That that Poppy you keep goin' on about, is it then?' He peers quickly at his reflection in the mirror. 'These stuck-up birds like a bit of rough, don't they?' Mick laughs at his own reflection and I laugh too.

'You like it at college then do you?' he says.

'No. Not really. Why?'

'Just asking. You still listening to that rap music crap then?'

'Yeah.'

'I don't see how you can understand what they're going on about. Must be some kind of black thing then, is it?'

'They're rapping in secret code,' I say. 'They're rapping about how much they want to kill all white people.'

We both crack up laughing.

I'm at the Hole In The Wall with a small bottle of gin tucked in the pocket of my new black bomber jacket. I'm with Pippa and four of the other Sloanes and we're on our way to a nightclub called Thursday's which is three miles outside of Chichester, in a village called Oving.

I am being chatted up by a man who looks old, old, old; he's got to be at least twenty-five, even thirty. The man keeps buying me drinks even though I'm already drunk.

He's a soldier at the army barracks in Chichester and he seems to have money galore. I don't fancy him at all but he's clearly interested in me and I'm kind of enjoying flirting with him. I'm trying on 'sexy'. It's unlike me to flirt. But suddenly it is making me feel powerful to be desired, even if the person doing the desiring looks like a cross between Freddie Mercury and Bruce Forsyth.

Poppy taps me on the shoulder.

'Stay away from that squaddie,' she whispers. 'He's married, and he's a right old lech.'

'Whatever,' I say.

I wonder whether Poppy's just jealous because I'm being chatted up by a mature, sophisticated dude.

The squaddie tells me his name and I instantly forget it. He tells me a joke that I don't get. Something about a girl taking it up the arse.

'Let me buy you another drink,' he says.

The gin has unlocked a new version of me, confident and full of herself. I've only ever drunk Diamond White, white wine or Bulmers cider before. I knock back more gin and watch myself becoming a different person. Throwing my head back, laughing when his jokes aren't all that funny.

The Sloanes make up excuses to leave for Thursday's without me. I know why: I'm a liability. I look young for my age and I'm the only one in our posse of sixteen-year-olds who doesn't have fake ID.

I ask the soldier what he thinks of the new LL Cool J single that, to my shocked delight is playing in the pub.

'LL what?' the soldier says.

I urgently need to pee, but the ladies loo is locked. The same girl has been in inside for forty minutes. I know this because I've been waiting to pee for all that time.

'She's probably in there with some bloke,' says the soldier. 'He's probably givin' her one in there.'

There's another toilet. A grimy public toilet, adjacent to the Hole In The Wall, just across the road from the Marks and Sparks car park where I loaded up Nanny's car with groceries earlier this evening. The soldier walks me out to the toilets. The building housing the toilets is made of dark bricks with a sign saying Gents on the left and one saying Ladies, on the right. He pushes me against the wall, in between the two signs, and he stares intently at me.

'You're fucking gorgeous,' he says.

'Really?'

I giggle and sway slightly as I approach the ladies' loos.

'You're pissed,' he says.

'So?'

He leans into me and manoeuvres me along the wall until we are in the doorway of the gents' loos. He keeps pushing me and I'm walking backwards, staggering really, until we're both inside the gents'. Feeling disorientated, I look around for a stall. There's one closed stall door and three urinals. A man wearing a long overcoat pisses into a urinal. The floor is strewn with dead cigarette butts and black smears of tar, and empty Durex and crisp packets.

The man in the overcoat glances at me, smirks, leaves.

I burp and the oily taste of the gin bubbles up into my throat making me feel nauseous and light-headed.

'I've got to sit down,' I say.

The soldier helps me sit down on the filthy floor and smooths my hair back with the palm of his hand and tips my chin up.

'You're fucking beautiful, do you know that?' He says

'Yeah I know it. Cos you already told me!'

I laugh. When I laugh my stomach churns up the alcohol coursing through my system and I feel not just light-headed now but quite out of control and out of my depth. It's time to ring my knight in tarnished armour, Cruising Capri Mick, from the phone box in the pub and sit there sobering up with a Diet Coke, waiting for him to arrive.

'Let's walk back to the pub,' I say. 'If I don't phone home soon my uncle's gonna come looking for me.'

'I thought you said you and your family lived all the way over in Fernmere?' the soldier says, looking amused. 'What's the hurry?'

'Can we just go back to the pub?'

'You look like you can hardly walk, sweetheart.'

'I'm fine.'

I scramble to get on to my feet and leave, but the soldier grips me round the waist from behind and pulls me to the lavatory floor. He clasps both wrists in one of his hands and pins me to the floor. He climbs on top of me and he stinks of sour BO and it feels like I've got a huge bundle of dirty laundry pressing down on me.

His voice is heavy in my ear, saying, 'Just a bit of fun. Come on.'

'I'm not really up for it,' I say, in a very small voice.

'Oh, come on,' he says. 'You're well up for it, aren't you? I know what you black girls are like: you love it.' A knowing laugh.

He keeps trying to put his knee between my legs to spread them but I keep my legs firmly closed as I try to sit up and push him away from me.

The new black lycra skirt from Dorothy Perkins that I am wearing barely grazes my thighs. Wendy's advised me to take the skirt back to the shop and exchange it for something decent.

My skirt's rucked up around the tops of my thighs and the soldier reaches up and yanks my knickers halfway down. I feel the filthy damp tiled floor against my bare skin.

'Fucking get off me.'

I try to sit up again and he knees me in the stomach and kneels on top of my lower body so that I can't move. I hear a zip being pulled and his penis is poking through his open flies, jabbing at my bare leg. The tip of it feels slimy against my skin. It triggers a memory from long-ago that rips through my body and emerges as a scream. I find my voice.

'NO! NO! I DON'T WANT TO!'

There are more words I want to say. I want to blame him for

every time I've been manhandled and forced to perform acts I didn't want to perform. I want to fight him. Hurt him. I'm certainly not going to let him hurt *me*. I'm sixteen and a half now. I can stand up for myself.

I wriggle out of his grip.

I'll run to the phone box just outside the loos and ring Cruising Capri Mick. If I tell Mick about this bastard trying to hurt me, Mick will come to Chichester, find him and kick his head in.

The soldier drags me back across the floor, pulling me closer to the urinals. He presses me onto my back, where I lay with my arms and legs flailing trying to flip myself over, get up and run away. He grabs a handful of my hair and my head slaps against the lavatory floor.

The soldier grins down at me. He pins me to the floor by pressing down on both of my shoulders with his hands, putting all his weight onto me.

'Get off of me!'

I feel his penis jabbing at my thighs, and then he is inside me and I cannot get away. My legs feel heavier than lead and I am not sure if I will ever be able to move from this lavatory floor.

'Aaaargh,' he says, grunting. 'Oh my fucking God you are so tight.'

He claws at my breasts through my bomber jacket. I lay on the floor with my legs prised apart and my knickers around my ankles. Something inside me is dying. I will realise, a few weeks from now, that the thing that's just died inside me on this lavatory floor is my will to live.

The scent of very stale piss, what smells like rivers of it, mingled with sharp disinfectant, fills my nostrils. I bring up a gut-full of vomit as he plunges into me again. I won't notice until tomorrow morning, but my hair and the left shoulder of my bomber jacket are covered in my vomit.

I will myself to leave the scene, to become a spectator only, watching with detachment as this man whose name I did not catch thrusts again and again into the me that's lying on the floor.

'Jesus Christ,' he says. 'Jesus *fucking Christ*.'

His words come out in ragged spurts. I am lying beneath a urinal. My head smacks against the tiled wall behind me, jolting me back into my body where I categorically do not want to be. Now I feel the pain; I feel like I am being broken, and crushed. The pain's not just in the part of my body he's plunging into but rather a deep, splintering ache and revulsion that resonate through my entire being.

This wouldn't be happening if I didn't deserve it, I think. It just wouldn't. I know I asked for it. By dressing like a tart and trying to look sexy. I shouldn't have grown so full of myself.

I watch him shudder and watch his eyes close and his face take on the look of a death mask. There's a sort of tortured grimace on his face. Like he's dying. Like somebody just shot him. I wish they had.

He grins and looks at me like he's expecting me to say something. What is there to say? In my world, this is what men do, and stupid me, buoyed up on gin, I had briefly forgotten this.

When the soldier leaves the men's loos, he says. 'I'll see you around, all right?'

At some point, I manage to get to Thursday's, smelling of vomit and gin. The bouncers demand ID and I just shove past them and run onto the dance floor. They're playing Tiffany's 'I Think We're Alone Now'. I whirl around the dance floor, looking for Poppy. I run to the ladies and lock myself into a cubicle where I down the rest of the bottle of gin I've still got in my jacket pocket. I slump forward on the toilet seat and begin vomiting again. A small sea of my vomit flows underneath the cubicle door. I close my eyes and drop the empty gin bottle onto the floor.

An echo-ing voice says, 'Oh my God.'

Someone hammers on the cubicle door, then kicks at it.

'Anita?' Pippa's voice.

'Can you just open the door, love?' someone else says.

The door seems to open by itself. I'm still hunched on the toilet. Crying. Someone in a uniform, a paramedic, I'm told later, says, 'If you'd had any more to drink, you would have had alcohol poisoning. You mightn't have made it.'

I wake up and I'm at home. And it's morning. Eight o'clock. I'm fully clothed on my bed and I've no idea how I got home. Nanny's left for her part-time job at the leisure centre, where she works in the crèche with Wendy as her boss. I fish out the pair of old gardening gloves that she keeps under the sink for the dirty jobs, like unclogging the drain. I put the gloves on and remove my clothes, item by item.

I toss my clothes into a bin liner, hide it in a corner of my wardrobe and lock myself in the bathroom. I run a bath, get in and immediately climb out again because I find that I can't sit in my own filth. My body is polluting the bath.

Our bathroom's tiny and I stand in the centre of it, in a trance, looking around me, jumping at my own shadow. The tiny window above the toilet is criss-crossed with cobwebs. I do not think I have ever disrobed in here before without Nanny needing to come in. She has to come in, because the water pills she takes force her to pee and pee and pee. Standing in front of the mirror, waiting for the bathwater to drain away, I look at my naked body and feel totally disconnected from it. When has my body ever felt like it truly belonged to me?

I slot in the shower attachment, grab my sponge and drag it repeatedly over my body as though I am scrubbing a filthy toilet. I toss the sponge into the bin, put my dressing gown on and sit in Nanny's chair by the window. Being in her chair makes me feel secure; the closest thing to getting a hug from her. I cannot ever tell Nanny what has happened because I fear she'd say 'Oh Nin, no,' and sit in silent judgement, crying. I don't think she'd hug me. I don't think she'd want to touch me.

I gaze vacantly through the window. A postman walks along West Walk. I've never seen him before – he must be new. He sees me through the window and stares, unblinking, not bothering to look away when I meet his gaze. I sink into Nanny's chair so that my head's beneath the window and I'm invisible. When I rise up again, the postman is standing there, looking worried and staring. It's not what you expect to see when you're delivering the post on Woodview: a black kid sitting in the window of someone's bungalow, clear as day. I sink down in the chair again and when I glance back up, the postman's gone.

I catch sight of my legs through the opening in my dressing gown and I want to vomit again. Even though I've scrubbed my legs so hard they look more pink than brown, I think I can still see the filth from the toilet floor and the soldier's semen seeping down them. I go to my room and put on a pair of opaque black tights under my dressing gown so that I won't have to see my revolting flesh.

I spend all day every day now in the college refectory, alone, reading Maya, reading Chester Himes and eating crisps; sneaking sips from miniature bottles of vodka and listening to Prince and LL Cool J on my Walkman. I no longer attend lessons. I'm afraid of interacting with anyone. The Sloanes say I've 'gone weird'. I feel safest when I'm alone.

A mixed-race student with beige skin and shoulder-length spiralling hair enrols and tries to introduce herself to me. When she asks what A Levels I'm doing, I tell her I'm doing English but that I can't remember the other subjects. Maybe Sociology? Politics? French? I can't remember. I've no idea.

Finally, I am called in to see the college principal. Nanny accompanies me, wearing her old cornflower-blue mac and a pair of navy leather driving gloves. The principal looks at me as though I'm a giant dog turd that's inexplicably found its way onto one of his office chairs. Nanny glares at him defiantly. Things are said, but I can't remember them now. I'm asked to withdraw from my course and I'm asked to stay off the college campus because my presence, my habit of wandering the corridors carrying a ghetto-blaster, my shameless boozing in the refectory, is distracting the other students.

One day, while I'm still using my free bus pass to lurk the streets of Chichester, I hit a new low. I've been sacked from my waitressing job at The Angel for not turning up for my shifts, Lloyds have retained my cashpoint card. I've been placed on some kind of blacklist by Littlewoods and Freemans and Kays for ordering jeans and jackets and trainers but failing to pay for them. No more clothes on the never-never. So I walk into a shop called Pilot, grab a bundle of clothes to try on, emerge from the changing rooms with an assortment of leggings and T-shirts hidden inside my coat and stroll out onto the High Street. I feel no remorse. I feel purposeful, in fact. Something precious was stolen from me, I'm stealing it back.

I'm seventeen when my mother and Agnes reappear. Aggy's getting married and Wendy and I are invited up to the wedding.

On the train to London, Wendy says, 'Don't you dare let your mother find out that you've dropped out of college. I'm not having her blaming me for the state you're in. I'm not having her running me down.'

For a second I consider telling Wendy what's really happening. That I'm free-falling and sinking and I have nothing to hold on to and no desire to hold on to anything anyway. Instead, I gaze listlessly out of the window. I can almost feel and taste Wendy's confusion and embarrassment at the state of me – not the state of my appearance but the poor quality of my attitude.

At the wedding Agnes tells me I look very grown up. I'm wearing a black shift dress I shoplifted from the Chichester branch of Next especially for the occasion. My mother approves of the dress, sidles up to me and tells me I look 'reasonably well turned out'.

My mother approves of Agnes's new husband too – a light-skinned freckly Nigerian man.

'I've no idea why he'd want to marry *Agnes*,' she says, grinning slyly. 'I bet the stupid girl is pregnant.'

I contemplate my mother as she says this, mesmerised by her heavily accented voice. I wonder what my mother looked like pregnant with me. I wonder whether she used to hold me and kiss me when I was a baby. Then I realise she didn't have the chance to do so, because she gave me up so soon after I arrived into the world. I want to tell my mother that, if she'd known me then, when I was newborn and clean and pure and plump, she could have loved me. I bet she could. If she'd given herself a chance. If she'd given *me* a chance.

I grab a glass of wine off a tray and gulp it down in mere seconds. Wendy, who's virtually teetotal, gives me a disapproving look so intense that I fear she might cry.

If Wendy's words are to be believed, I'm a waste of space and I'm rapidly becoming a disgrace to society. Nanny's far too indulgent, Wendy thinks. Nanny shouldn't let me sit around all day, doing sod all.

My handful of Fernmere friends are at work or still in the sixth form so I have nothing to do and nowhere to go so I stay at home with Nanny all day. Nanny seems vaguely glad of my company but she spends much of her time asleep in her blue armchair, by the window.

Mick manages to get me a job at the Grange as a cleaner, sweeping a smelly mop along the floor. It takes me two hours to clean one short corridor and I barely deserve to get paid.

At work one day, someone steals a fiver from someone's coat pocket in the men's changing rooms. Clearly I come across as the kind of girl who'd commit such a crime because the manager tells me, 'We can call the police and get the changing rooms fingerprinted.'

'Aren't valuables and cash supposed to be stored in lockers?' I say. 'If someone nicked his fiver, it's his own fault.'

I get the sack. But that's not a problem as Wendy's friend Tracey can put me forward for another job. Tracey's a huge woman with short, highlighted hair styled like Princess Di's, a huge slab of torso, the long turnip-shaped nose that seems to runs in her family plus arms bigger than my thighs – and my thighs aren't that small. Tracey works as a cleaner, sprucing up rich people's homes and she's so physically powerful that she can render a five-bedroomed house sparkling clean in forty-five minutes flat. She wants me to work with her as a sort of assistant cleaner.

Can't wait, I think.

'You know what your problem is?' Wendy says.

'No.'

'You think you're too good for a bit of honest hard work.'

I write to the *Fernmere Observer* asking for work experience. They write back asking me to come in for an interview. As I relay this news to Wendy, I'm stunned by the enthusiasm in my own voice.

'Work experience?' Wendy says. 'What you need is a proper job, love, and you need to hold on to it. I was working full-time by the time I was your age.'

'Good for you.'

'What's *wrong* with you?'

I shrug.

I honestly don't know what it is inside me that prevents me from remaining interested in anything; not in waitressing, not in being a chambermaid, working as a sales assistant at the bakery or boxing up cakes on the production line at the cake factory. I always stop turning up. Or I get sacked.

I try for secretarial work next because Nanny says it might be more up my street. I set up an appointment at a Chichester temping agency called Manpower. I go in wearing a navy blazer I nicked from Next, and a fake carefree-but-professional smile. The recruiter plucks out a card from her little plastic card file.

I recognise in a detached way, my value: I speak nicely, I wear smart (albeit stolen) clothes; and I can type.

'Let's put you forward for this one. It's temp-to-perm. They're looking for someone unflappable and well spoken,' the Manpower consultant says. 'That one's paying five pounds fifty an hour. You'll be typing, answering the phone and making coffee for the executives.'

'Great,' I say. I am genuinely thrilled at the prospect of five pounds fifty an hour.

I tell Wendy about my new job.

'Five pound fifty an hour doing what?' she seems both amused and deflated. 'What do you even know how to do? You barely know how to clean a sodding floor.'

'I'd be, like, a PA.'

'That's more than my Mick makes to support a whole family.'

'Well that's his problem, not mine.'

'I don't know who you flipping think you are, but I do know that you need to get off your high horse, madam.'

I'm not on any kind of high horse. How could I be when I'm a drop-out? The first day of my five-pound-fifty-an-hour temp-to-perm job arrives and I can't get out of bed. My legs feel so heavy that I'm unable to slide them out of bed and I remain there all day, staring at the ceiling.

Wendy comes around, enters my room uninvited and sits on the end of my bed for a talk. I can tell she's consulted her fat blond social worker friend Andrea, because she uses the sorts of words Andrea uses.

'I think you're clinically depressed. I think you're using drugs. Heroin.'

I begin to laugh. Heroin? I've never even smoked a cigarette.

'What the bloody hell are you laughing like that for?' says Wendy. 'I'm worried about you, Neet. I love you.'

I don't care whether Wendy loves me or not. I don't care whether anyone loves me, or not.

I keep hearing voices and they keep me awake all night. My head is filled to tipping-point with mocking words:

'I spent my life savings on you.'

'I *know* you black girls: you love it.'

'I wash my hands of you . . .'

'Your own mother doesn't even *like* you.'

I can only fall asleep at night if I knock back four or five or more cans of Special Brew at bedtime. Then eventually I'll pass out on top of my bed. One night I have an epiphany: I'm hearing voices and I'm drinking like a fish so clearly I have nerves. I wait until Nanny falls asleep in her armchair and slip into her bedroom and open the bottom drawer of her gold-edged chest of drawers. Among the sea of silver foil packets and brown glass bottles I find what I'm looking for. It feels soothing to steal something. To steal *anything*.

I soon see – or rather, feel – why Nanny likes her nerve pills so much. They're called Distalgesic and are part opiate and part paracetamol. I take thirty-eight of them, washed down with a lukewarm can of Special Brew. I dress in my African outfit and lay on my bed with my hands crossed over one another, on top of my chest. I don't want to die. I just no longer want to live the life I've been given.

Mick's got this button on his Atari computer that he can press and it shuts down and resets the machine's entire system. That's what I am trying to do to myself. This is not suicide. Suicide is surely wrought with melodrama and desperation, involving wrist-slashing or holding a gun to your head or hurling yourself off a tall building. But I just feel utterly at peace.

I fall into a velvety snooze, my mind feels like it's been cocooned in delicious softness and I am suddenly insulated from the anxiety that's been eating at me for months. For years, really. All of that friction, fear and worry evaporates, and I shut my eyes and let myself sink.

After 'what happened', as Nanny will come to call my overdose, she discovers what she fears is my dead body and rings Wendy. When Wendy rings 999, she's warned that I might die before an ambulance has time to weave its way from Chichester to Fernmere to collect me. It's quicker if Mick drives me into St Richard's hospital in the Ford Escort. I'm placed on the back seat. Wendy's in the passenger seat. Mick keeps taking his eyes off the road and turning round to watch me.

'Don't you go to sleep,' he says. 'Open your sodding eyes! Wendy! Make her open her eyes. I'm stoppin' the car!'

Mick is more animated than I have ever seen him.

My eyelids drop. A huge sense of spaciousness and peace opens like a rainbow inside me.

'Make her open her eyes Wendy!' says Mick.

He pulls over. Wendy slaps me lightly around the face.

'Neet, if you don't open your eyes, love. You might not ever wake up again,' she says.

'That's good,' I say.

'Why did you do it, love?' says Wendy.

I'm in a bed at St Richard's, with a tag taped round my wrist that says WILLIAMS, PRECIOUS ANITA. I've just had my stomach pumped.

'I'm sorry,' I try to say. My voice is faint, my throat feels battered, probably by the tube that was rammed down it last night.

'I just wanted to feel something,' I say.

The concerned smile slides off Wendy's lips.

'You what?' she says.

Mick's face slackens and crumples making him look like somebody who's been cheated in a game of cards but can't work out exactly how the deception occurred.

Nothing I am saying makes sense. Not even to me.

I can hear myself speaking and I can see myself thinking and trying to form the right words in my head but the words don't filter down into my mouth. What streams out sounds like a string of dream-talk, the sort of stuff I scrawl in my diary at night.

'I dunno,' I say, altering my accent. Aware of how incongruously posh my voice sounds reverberating around that bright white hospital room. I sound like Nanny. 'I dunno what made me do it.

I'm sent back home, and a couple of outpatient sessions with a psychiatric nurse are scheduled. I don't bother to turn up to see the psychiatric nurse because I decide before even meeting her that she won't be able to understand or help me.

'I'm off out for a walk, Nanny.'

The only time my head feels unclogged anymore is when I go for long walks by myself.

I've got my headphones on, listening to Public Enemy. I pull the door closed and plunge into the dusk. Nanny and I now live on the very edge of the estate, by a little path that runs past the fire station. Ours is the last of a strip of faded little bungalows created for the estate's elderly and infirm. Parked next to our bungalow, behind Nanny's Datsun, is an abandoned yellow car with foliage shooting through its broken windows.

Leaning against the rusty car is Keith, the hardest man on the whole estate. As I near him, I see that he's picking at the door of the car, and watching me. I try slipping straight past him but he follows me and stands in front of me, blocking my path. I pull off my headphones.

'What are you doing?' I say.

Keith smirks. He smells of dog's piss and wet fur. His mum, who he lives with when he's not in jail, breeds Jack Russells for a living. I try to step past him again and he jumps forward and blocks my path.

'What do you bloody want?'

I can't believe I've got the nerve to even look at this man, let alone argue with him. But something outside of myself is operating.

'I'm waiting for you, aren't I?' Keith says.

I study his face, trying to figure out what he's talking about and whether or not he's taking the piss. He'd be almost good-looking if it wasn't for the little mound of brown rot where one of his front teeth should be. He reminds me of Shakin' Stevens, but with longer, curlier hair.

'Why would you be waiting for me?'

'I need some help, don't I?' Keith says, eyeing me sceptically. 'We need someone nice-looking and that. As a sort of decoy. There's money in it. Thought you might wanna be in on it.'

Nice-looking – that's a bit of a stretch. Why would he single me out? Me, out of all the openly delinquent girls on our estate? It's not as if my shoplifting prowess is common knowledge. Does he suspect that as Woodview's only black girl I have a natural propensity towards crime?

Keith has been inside, for two long stretches, and he's proud of this. He went down for armed robbery the first time, GBH and possession of firearms the second. For Keith, sticking a rifle in somebody's face is all in a day's work. So how come he's talking to a nonentity like me?

I am flattered that he knows I even exist, that he knows exactly where I live. That he is standing here sizing me up, appraising me, and not in a sexual way but rather seeming to judge whether or not I've got the mettle to perpetrate crime at his level.

*   *   *

To be honest, I have little respect for the law now. I don't believe the law even applies to me anymore – it's never protected me, so why should I follow it? I have this malice and fury curdling inside me, making me see everything in a crude and simplistic way. I feel like lashing out. I'll never let anybody trample *me* like road kill again. It's my turn to hurt somebody, anybody, *everybody*. I want others to feel as frightened, as vulnerable, as *robbed* as I feel. As I have felt.

So, perhaps I really can and should do this, now – while the opportunity presents itself. Surely it's no coincidence that Keith has found me. I imagine the ring-ring of a till flying open. The fear in the shopkeeper's face. Keith's remorseless laughter as he realises we've pulled it off. Launching ourselves into a getaway car. A thick bundle of fifty-pound notes. Freedom. Redressing the balance.

'So, you up for it or not?' says Keith

I want to say yes. I want to say, 'Let's do it. Let's fucking do it.'

But I hesitate. Finally I squeak, 'But, why me?'

'Don't stress yourself, mate,' Keith says. 'I can find someone else. Just thought you might be up for it.'

Behind the abandoned car there's a tangle of blackberry bushes and then a drop down to a measly trickle of dirty shallow water that's supposed to be a stream. I look down into the filthy water. I look up at Keith, without quite meeting his gaze.

'I'd better not do it,' I say.

'I'd better not,' he mimics, thrusting his hands in his jeans pockets, squaring his shoulders and walking away.

I shrug and put my headphones back on: Public Enemy – 'Rebel Without A Pause'. It's not that I'm against being – or continuing to be – a badgirl crim, *per se*. It's just that I want to keep all my options open.

It's just that I want to go to London.

Paid In Full

I EMERGE FROM BRIXTON tube station carrying an Adidas holdall containing an LL Cool J cassette tape, bras, knickers, a spare tracksuit and a toothbrush. I have twelve pounds in my pocket, and no plan at all, other than to hang around with black people and maybe find a way to get into journalism.

I'm met at the station by Effua, my former foster-sister. Effy wrote to me, sending me her address and a recent photo. I have written to her telling her I'm coming to London. Here I am.

There's a record shop by the tube station exit. A Rastaman in a camouflage jacket leans in the doorway of the shop. His dread-locks are impenetrably thick, spiralling from his head in a gravity defying brown and black mane. His eyes sweep over me, lingering on the picky ends of my matted hair. When he looks away, into the flowing rush-hour crowd, I stand there transfixed, unable to move past him and his hair.

'I *love* his hair,' I whisper to Effy. 'How do you get it like that? Is that, like, hair extensions?'

'Man,' says Effua, shaking her sleek head. 'You've got a lot to learn.'

Effua's mum, Aunty Akosua, has a shop in Brixton market. There's African material hanging up in sheets. Wrinkled brown ladies sitting in fold-up chairs – chattering and slurping down mashed boiled plantain. Through the open door I feel reggae playing so loud it makes the pavement shudder. I try to etch the hustle of the market into my memory because I know Wendy will ask me about it, the way she always does when I see something she doesn't get to see.

Then I remember. I don't live in Fernmere anymore. I've said my goodbyes. I called Wendy from a phone box at Waterloo and said, 'I know you won't understand but I've got to go. I'm sorry. I do love you.'

'It'll break Nanny's heart,' Wendy said. 'It'll break Mick's heart.'

Why didn't Wendy say it would break her heart too? I'd asked myself, as I bought a tube ticket and slipped underground.

Half an hour in London and I feel alive, I'm shaken awake by the sights and sensations I've been longing for all my life without even realising how hard I was longing. Everywhere I turn there are b-boys clutching ghetto blasters, black kids in Adidas shell-toes with fat white laces. Stalls selling hair-grease, plantains, yams, 12-inches of LL Cool J and Lisa Lisa tracks. Even the shuddering London buses enchant me. In Fernmere our buses come once every two hours and only go to Hampshire, Surrey or deeper into Sussex. Here the bright red buses appear every second and shoot off to Notting Hill, Oxford Street, Victoria, Peckham . . .

'How is your mother?' Aunty Akosua asks.

'I've no idea,' I say, my voice a monotone.

'Is she still living in Belsize Park?'

'I don't know.'

My mother has kept the promise she made when I was eleven. Aside from the two-minute conversation at Agnes's wedding, she has had absolutely nothing to do with me. She's washed her hands of me and moved on. Agnes has followed her lead.

Aunty Akosua gives Effy and me a tenner to spend at McDonald's. As we munch Big Macs, Effua says, 'We've got nuff catching up to do. Can you stay the night with us?'

I'm staying much longer than that, I think.

*   *   *

I stay at Aunty Akosua's council flat, on the twelfth floor of a Catford high rise. Weeks drift by. I'm an uninvited but constant presence. Aunty Akosua doesn't seem to mind me, but she screams all day and night at Effua, criticising her virtually every time she moves or breathes. Effua says she wishes she'd been allowed to stay in Fernmere with Wendy and Mick for ever. She reminisces daily about her time there, about the endless days out to the zoo and to the seaside, the expensive dolls Mick used to buy us. About being allowed to eat candy floss *and* ice cream *and* toffee apple all in the same day. Only white people treat kids that softly, she says.

Aunty Akosua is tough with Effua, but quite gentle with me, offering me advice I didn't even ask for, stroking my ego with compliments and encouragement. She even says she wishes I was her daughter. My mother, she says, was a 'classy' and 'extremely intelligent' lady and I'd do well to follow in her footsteps. I'm shocked anyone would have the nerve to suggest such a thing. Wouldn't following in my mother's footsteps entail beating people up and constantly letting them down?

'What do you mean about following in my mother's footsteps, Aunty?' I ask warily.

'Your mother was an accountant, my dear. Why don't you go into accounting? You've got the brilliance. Unlike *her*,' she adds, jerking her thumb at Effua, who sits there giving us screwface, pretending not to feel her mother's disappointment.

I hadn't realised my mother *really* had a proper job. Nanny had told me, often, that my mother's so-called job in some grand offices up in London was probably just a figment of her imagination.

There's Effy, Effy's all-girl crew and me, me the strangely stiff, shaggy-haired girl from the country. I'm relieved that Effua's friends don't actually laugh at me. But then they daren't laugh, because Effua approves of me and Effua, after all, is at the juicy epicentre of all that's cool around here. You can't fuck with her.

Jobless and broke and underage, we roam the streets of Catford and Peckham and Brixton, batting ideas back and forth, dreaming up new ways to nick things from shops without getting busted. Effua says I need to do something about the way I talk. So I try to. I try to spice my accent up and at the same time tone it down. Make it lazier and less crisp. Absorb Brixton speech patterns and remember to say *nah* instead of no and *I'm vex* instead of *I'm fed up*.

I continue to sound just like Nanny.

Eventually I relax and just work with what I've got. Here, at large in Lambeth, I have a natural edge when it comes to perpetrating petty scams, issuing rubbery cheques and making off without payment. People (checkout girls, store detectives, bank clerks) have higher expectations of someone who sounds like me. They're likelier to give me the benefit of the doubt. I delight in letting each and every one of them down.

In Morleys and in Boots and the Body Shop, it is me who goes up to the till and asks endless inane questions to distract the checkout girl while the rest of the crew stuff their pockets with the swag. We gloat over our latest spoils in Taneesha's bedroom in Catford. We sit in a circle, passing around two bottles of Thunderbird. Everyone's taking it in turns to rap a freestyle verse. Everyone apart from me.

I watch Effua. Her cheekbones looking like they're constructed out of steel. Skin darker than Bournville chocolate. Hair greased down just right with Ultra Sheen. She spits out a rhyme about a local boy and how there's no way she's ever gonna get with him because he's so *dry*.

I bop my head and quake inside, dreading my turn. Will I have to rap about the sheep and goats and cows in Fernmere? I swig Thunderbird and pass the bottle to Debra. I'm preparing to pretend I that I'm suddenly too mashed up to even speak, so that

I can get out of this. But when it's my turn to rhyme, everyone acts like I'm not really there.

This is how I dreamed life in London would be. It does not occur to me that there may be more involved in being black than tearing around south London, stealing. I am in love. Not in love with a bloke but with this lifestyle I've found where we speak our own language made up of Americanisms and phrases plucked from rap verses. Where we listen to hip-hop from a.m. to p.m., and we own twenty pairs of Nikes and Adidas each. And we make believe we have links to New York and talk about hip-hop's birthplace, the South Bronx, like we've been there.

In years to come I will meet many of the men, and women, whose voices and stories, whose poetry, so inspired me and gave me such hope and meaning, such a rich sense of connectedness. Rakim and LL Cool J and MC Lyte and Run DMC and Big Daddy Kane. I will travel to New York to interview them for magazines and I will sit opposite or beside them, pretending to be cool and composed while inside I am silently screaming, *I made it! I did it!*

I still don't look as fly as my peers and that's mainly because of my hair, which I don't have the money to get sorted out just yet. My nickname's 'Pickyhead' – not really a good start. The rest of the girls in our crew wear asymmetrical straightened hairstyles like Salt-N-Pepa's. I try to keep up. I've got the huge rectangular fake gold door-knockers dangling from my ears. And I wear the home-made trousers shaped like MC Hammer's parachute pants that the b-girls all wear. The ones made from African material scammed from Brixton market that someone's mum runs up on her sewing machine. Elastic bands looped around the ankles and then the trousers billow out in the wind.

Every boy I bump into at one of Effy's mates' houses – or

make shy eye contact with in the street – looks almost as dope as Big Daddy Kane or Slick Rick. The boys shine, literally, in white shell suits and glimmering shoulder-padded suits the colour of knife blades. They wear huge thick ropes of gold or fake gold around their necks and the proper bad boys have diamond-encrusted four-finger gold rings that stretch across their hands like precious knuckledusters. The whole vibe is sharp and jagged, right down to their hair which is shorn to grade-one at the back, shaped to a tall tilt in the centre and scored with tramlines at the sides.

The most important emblem of all is a green, yellow, red and black leather pendant strung on a long black chord, bearing an outline of Africa. I buy mine (after an abortive attempt to nick it) from Four Star General on Oxford Street.

The day I slip my Africa pendant around my neck, I feel more disconnected from Africa than I ever have before in my life. As a child my mother constantly droned on about me being Nigerian. Here, in the late eighties, in London, we UK-born Africans wear Africa pendants but don't truly embrace the message. Speak with an African accent, show any African idiosyncracy at all, and hear your peers hiss 'shame!' But I feel black, I think. Whatever that is. According to the group the Jungle Brothers, black is black is black is black.

One day something new stirs within me. Or perhaps it is not something new exactly, but rather an itch, a desire that has lain dormant for a time. I am missing the days in school, when my English teachers lavished me with praise. I'm craving that delicious tingle of smugness I'd feel when a teacher handed me back my homework with an A scrawled at the top of the page in red pen. I want to be seen, once again, as the foster-kid who just might have a surprisingly bright future.

To hear Effua tell it, 'A bitch is selling out.'

*　　*　　*

My selling out begins with a job interview. I purchase a copy of the *Evening Standard*. I've been considering ringing up the editor of the *Standard* and asking him or her for a job as a trainee reporter. I picture myself writing features about hip-hop culture. Before I make the call, a job ad in the back pages of the paper catches my eye. A situation is vacant for an accounts clerk at a travel firm in EC1. Didn't Aunty Akosua say something about my mother being an accountant?

The company's called Gulliver's Travel Agency. At the interview I say, 'I've always been extremely good with figures. I come from a long line of accountants.'

'Is that so?' says the man interviewing me – an accountant named Simon.

I tell Simon I've just turned eighteen, which is true and that I've just passed A Level maths, which obviously isn't. Surprisingly I pass an on-the-spot maths test.

'Ever since I was a child, I've always been obsessed with numbers,' I say. 'You couldn't get me to write anything or read a book. All I did was play with calculators, do sums in my head. People used to nickname me Figures . . .'

The lies pour forth. I listen to myself as if from afar. I sit there thinking sell-out, sell-out, sell-out.

Simon uses phrases the career advisor at my school used to use, such as 'You'll receive on-the-job training' and 'There's room for growth and promotion.'

He can start me on a salary of £8,000 a year. I'll start on Monday. I'll be able to put myself forward for exams, which, if I pass them, will transform me into something called an Accounting Technician. From there, apparently, the sky's the limit as far as accounting goes.

Life as a Junior Accounts Clerk in the City is so soulless and unchanging that it's almost funny. And yet I turn up on time, day after day after day, breathlessly reliable like a ticking clock.

I'm modelling myself after a nugget of advice Mick gave me when I first became a drop-out. 'Holding down a job builds your character, dunnit?'

But despite my extreme reliability, I feel constantly on edge as a Junior Accounts Clerk. Like something bad is about to happen. The numbers on my VDU screen make my head contract and ache. The figures on the sheets of paper I keep being fed look like code to me.

Perhaps it's my own fault I feel on edge. By the end of my second month at my new job, I've told my new colleagues so many lies about my life that it's no longer possible to indulge in normal conversation even, in case I give myself away. I've claimed to have a mum and dad, who are married (to each other) and with whom I live. I said it all because I wanted to fit in. As the only black girl in the office besides the cleaner, I felt a need to seem ultra respectable and ultra likeable. And normal.

Now that I've got a job, I'm able to get a room of my own: in a flat-share in Brixton, on Coldharbour Lane. I rent the room from a posh white woman called Jane. She's older than me and from Chichester. I've no idea what she thinks she's playing at living on the frontline in Brixton.

At the interview for the flat-share, Jane says – her voice rich with surprise and delight – that I am 'so well spoken'. She wants to know what my parents do and where I went to school. I claim to have attended a well-known Catholic boarding school. And my dad works in oil, I say. My mother's a maths professor at Oxford.

Jane tells me the room's mine if I want it.

Effy's not impressed.

'You're fucking watchin' Channel Zero,' she screams. 'You've lost it.'

And our friendship fizzles out in much the same way it originally began, back when we were toddlers duelling for Nanny's love. A vicious argument, then a punch-up and mutual hair-pulling and scratching outside Peckham Rye station, leaving me suddenly friendless and with a small bald patch on one side of my head.

Jess, a friend from Fernmere Grammar School, moves to London to work as a PA in the West End. The two of us take up raving. Incredibly, nobody has the heart to openly laugh at our lame dance moves and we spend several nights a week in the West End, trying our hardest to dance, right through until dawn. And that's when I meet the boy.

The boy is swaggering to and fro outside the Limelight night-club in Piccadilly. Handing out flyers for an upcoming rave in Deptford. He has fresh tramlines etched into the sides and back of his head and he's wearing a white-and-yellow shell suit that reminds me of a parachute. He calls himself MC Hassan. He looks me up and down and inclines his head in such a way that it's clear he thinks I'm attractive. Jess gives me that nudge in the ribs that means, 'You've pulled.'

'You. You look like Bola,' says MC Hassan.

'What's Bola?'

'She's just a friend, innit. She's pretty. Like you. You Nigerian?'

'I guess so.'

'You *guess* so? You need to claim your culture! Igbo, yeah?'

'How did you know?'

MC Hassan winks at me.

'You ever been back home? Nigeria?'

'When I was a kid.'

'How old are you now?'

'Old enough.'

He laughs a little and fiddles with the massive ring on his finger.

'I knew you were Nigerian. Word.'

For reasons I cannot explain I agree to accompany MC Hassan back to his council flat in New Cross Gate. He says we've got a lot to talk about. He says he can see that I need schooling about my culture. As far as I'm concerned my culture is hip-hop and I don't need schooling in it. I know everything about it.

I sit on his tatty sofa with my arms wrapped tightly around my body. There's no heating, but I'm too shy to admit I'm cold.

'You all right?' he says.

'I'm fine, thanks.'

'I've seen you around.'

I arch an eyebrow.

'You hang out with that white girl, innit?' Hassan says. 'Yeah, what's up with that girl? She's been all over the estate.'

He's talking about Jess. Ever since she moved to London, Jess has become obsessed with black blokes. She seeks them out when we go raving – or rather they find her. Jess's blond whiteness shimmers like a beacon on dance floors packed tight with black bodies. Black homeboys make a beeline for her, sauntering and doing the running man across sweaty dance floors to get next to her.

As if Jess's blonde beauty wasn't enough, she also has me at her side: I'm, like, her visual affirmation, a walking, talking reminder to anyone watching that Jess is down with black peeps.

'I couldn't even get it up for a white girl, you get me?' says Hassan.

I don't get him actually. I hear what he says but I don't see how it can be true. So far I've not met a black guy who didn't, on some level, seem to rate white girls higher than black ones. It's not clear to us black girls why this is but it is just how it is. And the black boys who can't pull white chicks often go for mixed-race girls instead, the ones with tea-toned skin and long bubbly hair.

I've heard it's different in America. I've heard that LL and Kane *only* go out with black girls. But here in England, it seems girls who look like me, we're the boobie prize, the bottom of the barrel. Nobody's first choice, ever. But Hassan swears he only fancies Nubian sisters, which means that by default he must fancy me more than he fancies Jess. I try to take this all in. It doesn't seem to add up. I feel like I just won the pools, like a prize I don't deserve and didn't even compete for just dropped into my lap.

Hassan hands me a bundle of flyers depicting Alsatians' heads superimposed onto human bodies wearing raincoats. The dog-headed bodies in the picture are jostling along a train platform carrying briefcases.

'It's white people, innit?' Hassan says. 'Blue-eyed devils.'

'The things in the picture are dogs. Alsatians.'

'It's what white people are, innit.'

'You're saying that white people are actually dogs? You're a fucking nutter, man!'

Hassan says he belongs to an organisation I've never heard of, called The Nation of Islam.

'White people,' he says, 'are devils.'

'What?'

'Blue-eyed devils.'

I giggle.

'This ain't no joke.'

'Why would you say such evil things?' I'm ready to get up and leave.

'Don't ever. Don't *ever* call a black man evil. Whites are evil. Blue-eyed devils. They're snakes. You can't trust any of them. They'll trick you. They'll always betray you.'

His deep, hypnotic voice begins to coax and persuade me. I start to think Hassan perhaps, maybe, possibly has a point. The way I see things, white people have let me down, assaulted me, ruined my life. I don't think of my mother as having abandoned me; I think of Nanny as having stolen me from my mother. Images of white people flash before me: the white soldier in the gents' toilets. Nanny telling me to run away when my stepfather came to collect me for a visit.

This, I decide, is surely what I came to London for; to be a part of something *exclusively* black.

'I want to join it,' I say.

'Join what?'

'The People of Islam.'

'You mean The Nation, yeah?'

'Yeah.'

'You've got a lot to learn before I can take you to the mosque.'

Hassan never does take me to the Nation of Islam mosque. Presumably I never learn enough. Eventually he drops out of the Nation himself. A decade later, fresh from a postgraduate journalism course, I approach the Nation of Islam and tell them I'd like to write an article about them. I am not the only journalist interested. There is a high-profile inquiry underway into Stephen Lawrence's murder. Men from the Nation of Islam show up at the inquiry, immaculately turned out in black suits and red bow ties. National newspapers are running headlines asking, 'Nation of Islam – who are they?'

My interview request will be denied: a Nation spokesman will ask me, 'Why should we care what the white media thinks of us?'

I decide then to join the Nation of Islam, under an assumed name. I spend about a week in the Nation. I ring up *The Times'* features desk and say, 'You don't know me but I've got a story I think you might want to have a look at.' The media's been slating the Nation as wholly sinister and racist but I explain the strong elements of self-discipline and self-respect they teach. *The Times* will bite and even though I have no cuttings to prove I've got what it takes, they publish my 3,000-word piece about life and training for women in the Nation in their Saturday magazine a couple of weeks later.

'So what ends you from? Where'd you grow up?' asks Hassan.

And what do I do? I only go and mess everything up by letting it slip that I was brought up by a white woman. In West Sussex. I presume Hassan will jump to his feet and usher me out of his flat. Instead he becomes (even more) animated at this news.

'*Is it?*' he says. 'My cousin Kemi was fostered by whites innit? In Horsham. She was lost, so lost. Lost! They'd brainwashed her into thinking whites were better than blacks. You remind me of her, innit? She came to London, hooked up with me and her other cousins and now she's rejuvenated. Re-educated. Rejuvenated. Re-educated.'

I find myself wanting to be rejuvenated and re-educated too.

'I was fostered myself by a white woman in Essex, you get me?' he reveals suddenly.

'Don't take the piss.'

'Word is born, I was fostered. Only for a year though innit.'

'What was your foster-family like then?'

'Not that bad as far as things go. But I was miserable. Miserable. I was so sad and felt so isolated that I couldn't stop eating sweets. I got so fat. I put on so much weight. By the time I was ten I had a thirty-six-inch waist!'

There's a spark, a connection made. I feel as though I'm a jigsaw puzzle, made of fragments, and that only now are the pieces of me being slid into place. I'm finally, in this moment, at ease. And I mistake shared experience for instant love. This is the man I am going to marry, I think to myself.

I return to Hassan's flat three days later wanting more, but not at all sure what I'm wanting more of. He asks me what I think I know about hip-hop. As well as owning over a hundred hip-hop LPs, he also does a bit of rapping at raves, and presents a community radio show. Hassan's favourite group is Public Enemy. I say I like NWA better but that 'Don't Believe the Hype' is one of the best tracks I've heard in my life.

He begins firing questions at me, about rappers and the true meanings of their names.

'D'you know what KRS-One stand for?' he asks.

'Knowledge Reigns Supreme Over Nearly Everyone.' I fire back.

'What does the KANE part of Big Daddy Kane stand for?'

'King Asiatic Nobody's Equal.'

Hassan looks impressed.

'All right, all right. Who invented hip-hop?'

'Kurtis Blow.'

'Wrong!' he says, leaping up from the sofa. 'It's DJ Kool Herc!'

At seventeen, Hassan's six months younger than me. Like me, he started his A Levels but quickly dropped out. The white education system couldn't teach him *nothing*. His parents moved back to Nigeria without him when he was only sixteen and that's when he got his own council flat. We've been chatting for about an hour when I tell him that I think I am in love with him.

'Nah,' he says. 'How can you be? You hardly know me.'

Soon Hasssan's entire tower block, and other blocks surrounding it, will be condemned by Southwark Council and bulldozed into dust. All I notice about his flat is that it is dark and that there is no bed, only a mattress on the floor. I'm on that mattress, laying flat on my back. Unmoving.

'You wanna do, you know – thingie? Yeah?'

'I dunno. I guess so.'

'OK then,' says Hassan.

'OK.'

'Big girl, innit,' he says, trying to pull my jeans down. I lay there, unwilling to part with any of my clothes. I'm not necessarily against having sex with him but I hang on tightly to my clothes, too ashamed of my body to want it to be seen naked. Like he said, I *am* a big girl. I'm tall, just over five foot nine now and I weigh nearly eleven stone because I eat at least five packets of crisps a day, not to mention the heaping plates of fried plantains I consume for breakfast and dinner.

I close my eyes. Hassan strokes my face and my hair and fumbles underneath my sweatshirt in search of my breasts. I lose the jeans but keep the sweatshirt on. It's a blue hooded sweatshirt with the Coca-Cola logo emblazoned across the chest. Nanny bought it for me for my seventeenth birthday and she spent half a week's pension on it.

I lie still. Clench my jaw. Why is this taking him so long? A year and a half ago the soldier can't have taken more than three minutes. I was showing a reaction then though; that must have been it. I was screaming and trying to get away and not just lying still like a corpse.

This feels like a trip to the dentist. Being eased back till you're horizontal. Laying there waiting for the dreaded thing to begin. Teeth gritted. And it's uncomfortable but not quite as horrid as you'd feared. In the end, it's over much quicker than you'd imagined it would be.

Later, Hassan provides a commentary on my non-performance. 'You needed to, you know, open your legs more. Or move around more.'

'Yeah. Sorry.'

All I keep thinking is: *Hassan didn't force me.* I made the decision to do it with him. If I'd said no, he'd have respected that and let me go.

So does this mean that from now on I have a say in what happens to my body?

Contraception isn't discussed. I know that the Pill exists but all I've been told about it is that you only need to go on it if you're a married woman or you're an unmarried scrubber. I know about Durex, aka 'rubber johnnies'. Learned about those from an embarrassed Mr Farrell, my Biology teacher at school. The day he tackled the facts of life and showed us slides of wombs and childbirth, the boys sniggered so loudly that nobody could hear much of what was being said.

Not that contraception is really needed in my situation. I've *had* sex with Hassan but I'm not going to be having it again. There's no way I can ever see Hassan anymore because, I mean, what if I go round there and he expects to shag me *again*? It's nothing personal against him, it's just that now I've finally done it (voluntarily) I find the whole thing, the very idea of sex, unsettling; sort of frightening and frighteningly familiar all at the same time.

Less than three weeks pass before I realise something is very, very wrong. I keep crying for no reason at all. Aromas I adore, like freshly ground coffee and freshly laundered clothes, start to nauseate me. It feels like the weird symptoms I get the week before my period, but exaggerated. Plus my period due date swings by and there's no period, just more mood swings, more aversion to nice smells and drama-queen tears.

I scrape together the cash to buy a Clearblue kit from Superdrug. Then I ring up Jess at her flatshare.

'What are you gonna do?' she says, holding my hand, staring at the plastic testing stick on my dressing table.

I shrug. 'Nothing, I guess.'

'So you're gonna have the baby?'

'Of *course* not.'

'So you're gonna have an abortion then?'

'Ewww. No. Are you on *crack*?'

I tell myself it makes sense to just pretend this is not really happening. I can simply forget about it, like I've forgotten about other scary things, and it will go away all by itself.

One evening, on my way home from work, I bump into Effua at Brixton tube station. She sucks her teeth at me at first but eventually we both crack up laughing and we hug and my secret comes spilling out and I begin to cry.

'Calm down,' says Effua. 'Have the baby, innit? Get on the housing list, get a flat. Then check the next guy.'

Nobody asks me who the father is. I wonder what Jess is thinking. I've never in my life had a boyfriend. I've shown so little interest in dating that I think some of my Fernmere peers fear I am a lesbian. Or is Jess assuming I've had a secret life all these years and that I've shagged so many guys that I've no idea which one it was?

* * *

I spend the first two hours of each working day in the loos puking up. I begin to show up at Gulliver's later and later in the mornings until, several days later, I am sacked.

I keep picking up the phone and dialling Nanny's number and when I hear her say, 'Hello. Hello. Nin, is that you?' I hang up.

Eventually, I ring Wendy. The words tumble out of my mouth.

'It's me. I'm sorry I haven't been in touch for so long Wendy but I need your help. I think I might need to have an abortion or something.'

'What are you on about, love?'

'I'm pregnant, Wendy.'

'You're what? Blinkin' hell, love. Are you all right?'

'No.'

The next day Wendy arrives with Mick in the Ford Escort.

'What you wearing then?' Mick says, grinning and then kissing me on the cheek.

I'm wearing African print genie pants that puff out wildly at the ankles and big Fila trainers. My Africa pendant's slung around my neck.

Wendy says, 'You look awful, love.'

I've packed my tracksuits, LPs and my twenty-two pairs of trainers into three black bin liners. Mick won't let me carry anything.

'Can't let a pregnant lady exert herself, can we?' he says, hauling my bin bags into the boot of the car. 'What you go and get yourself knocked up for then? Bloody idiot.'

Nothing more is said. There's nothing to say. I turned my nose up at them, turned my back on them and now I'm asking Wendy and Mick for help and I've no idea how much help they're prepared to give me beyond driving me back to Fernmere and depositing me in Nanny's bungalow.

On the voyage home, Mick zig-zags to the wrong side of the road every now and then just to make Wendy scream and then get cross and go, '*Don't Mick*,' every time. I watch listlessly through the window as the car careens across the road. I feel ungrateful and afraid and relieved and confused.

We drive into Fernmere. It's just past twilight and the streets are almost empty. I feel as if I'm being nudged gently into a warm tomb while still alive. There's a sense of descending, of sinking and it's making my stomach flutter inside. Then I realise the feeling in my stomach is my baby kicking.

Easy

'EIGHTEEN WEEKS,' SAYS THE doctor. 'It's not too late.'

I'm lying on my back with my legs spread and my feet high above me in stirrups, trying desperately not to throw up. The doctor's contempt is palpable, rising from him like toxic vapour as he peers down at me, the latest in a long line of teenaged, unwed mothers-to-be to hail from Woodview.

I feel like a giant slug, lying there and taking it. Listening to other people talk about what I should do and shouldn't do. Feeling strangely mute, unable to say or even decide what I want. I am eighteen, a woman finally. So why am I skulking around like a young child, craving Nanny and Wendy's approval like an addict chasing a fix? Why am I waiting for somebody to save me, to take me by the hand or even grab me by the hair, and tell me what to do?

I listen intently to what Wendy and Nanny say. Wendy says it's my decision what I do about the pregnancy but that she doesn't see the point in me having the little darling only to have it adopted by strangers.

Nobody seems to want to broach the subject of abortion.

Until, that is, my mother finds out I'm preggers.

The entire time I lived in London, I didn't look up my mother. I couldn't anyway as I didn't have her address. Then, when I am up in London with Jess, meandering along Oxford Street, there's this black woman hovering outside Selfridges. She's so lavishly built she could serve as a ship's figurehead. She clutches bulging Selfridges carrier bags in one hand and waves for a taxi with the other. The woman stares and stares, so intensely that I to avert my curious eyes.

I tug at Jess's elbow. 'See that woman there? Why's she staring at me like that? Oh my God, she's fucking coming over!'

The woman glides over, hips rolling.

'Who are you?' she demands. 'I know you!'

She has a heavy Nigerian accent, stirring a remembrance deep within me. A memory of my mother and the disparaging words she used to lob at me like darts.

I look at the woman and ask, 'Who are you?'

'Aieeeee!' says the woman. 'Precious! It's my little Precious! Look at you! I'm your Aunty Onyi!'

It has been ten years. I have grown substantially taller. Aunty Onyi has grown substantially wider. She draws me into an Anaïs Anaïs-scented hug and then steps back to check me out.

'Precious, you are looking *fine*,' Aunty Onyi, eyeing the formidable bust-line jutting through my mac, the only outward indication of my condition.

'I'm pregnant.'

'Precious!' she says. 'Pregnant? How is that possible? How old are you now?'

'Old enough.'

Aunty Onyi tells my mother, of course.

My mother rings me up at Nanny's.

'How did you become pregnant?' she screams.

'I had sex.'

'If you take that attitude I am going to hang up this phone.'

'OK. I *apologise*.'

'I'll pay for you to have an abortion at a private clinic. You can come to London.'

'I don't know what I want to do yet.'

'Neety! What is going to happen to your life if you don't get rid of this? I suppose those sick idiots in Fernmere are brainwashing you into keeping it, so they can have another Nigerian baby to add to their collection. Unless you have an abortion, you're finished. I'll wash my hands of you.'

Haven't you already washed your hands of me? I think.

'I suppose you're scared of becoming a grandmother,' I say.

'I'm already a grandmother. Your sister had a daughter last year.'

Agnes. I ask my mother where my sister is. How old Agnes's baby is. I ask her for Agnes's phone number.

'I don't have any number,' my mother claims. 'But if I do find it, I will give it to you when you come up to London to come to the clinic.'

She hangs up.

'My mother says I have to have an abortion,' I tell Wendy and Nanny. I feel almost relieved that a grown-up has finally made a decision for me. 'Do you think I should have one?'

Nanny says, 'She's got some nerve telling you to have an abortion, Nin. What on earth has any of this got to do with that selfish bloody bitch?'

Wendy tells Nanny to calm down and says that if I *do* want to have an abortion, it's up to me. It's my body. She's not comfortable with the idea of it, neither is Mick. But it's my choice, she says.

When Wendy's not around to overhear, Nanny whispers anti-abortion rhetoric into my ears. She tells me a story about an aborted foetus that lived through the abortion and was found screaming, mangled and striving to draw breath on the hospital floor.

'The nurses can't stand being involved in abortions,' she says. 'They think it's wrong and they're none too gentle with the girls who go in for it. You can't really blame them, can you, Neet?'

No, I can't blame them. I can't blame anybody but myself. I still don't know what to do. My GP is more than happy to refer me for an abortion but I am afraid of making a choice. I don't feel qualified to make such a portentous decision. Who am I to abruptly snuff out a potential life just because I am too stupid and too immature to really know what's best?

I sit in the armchair opposite Nanny, wondering if Nanny would come and pick me up in her car after the abortion, should I end up having one. Or would that be it? Would Nanny want nothing further to do with me?

Would Wendy come to the hospital with me and sit there smiling bravely while I was spreadeagled with my feet up in stirrups? Would she hold my hand while I was scraped out extra-hard by a disapproving nurse whose eyes told me I deserved every second of pain. I think of blood spurting like a fountain. Of a jelly-like mass of butchered foetus slithering out onto the hospital floor.

Nanny sees me grimace.

'Someone just walk over your grave, Nin?' she says.

The weeks tick by. The pregnancy continues by default. I'm too dissociated to fully embrace what's happening. There isn't a moment where I say, 'Nanny, Wendy, I've got something to tell you. I've decided to have the baby.'

Another day, another doctor. This one smears a sperm-like jelly across my belly. Wendy and Nanny grin down at me, their smiles exaggerated and ghoulish. 'Look, Neet! Can you see? Look at the screen Neet! Can you see, love?'

All at once, I am treated as if I'm spun from rare silk. Not only by Wendy and Nanny but also by our neighbours and friends on the estate. Between them, the folks around me get me kitted out, materially, for motherhood. They donate Babygros, a cot and bottle sterilising kits and buy me baby blankets and quilt sets with a generosity that astounds me. My bedroom fills up with Mothercare accessories and I am caught up in a whirlwind of shopping and support and acceptance. Never in my life have I felt so loved and so approved of. Getting knocked-up young is what girls on our estate do. Finally, I fit in.

During the day, we shop for prams and baby baths and cots and Babygros. At night, I have a recurring nightmare where I find myself in the middle of a swamp, sinking. I scream for help and Nanny and Wendy wade in and stand there, holding my hand as we're all sucked in by the swamp. 'We are here with you, Neet,' Wendy says.

'I won't ever leave you,' Nanny says.

I remain sullen and sulky and overwhelmed. Wendy and Nanny make plans on my behalf. There seems to be an unspoken assumption that my baby won't be wholly mine – he or she will be *ours*. My main role, perhaps, is to be the vessel doing the delivering, bearing the fruit. Wendy suggests I take in a short-term African foster-child for a bit, to learn hands-on how to hold and bathe a baby, how to change nappies and how to mix up formula.

'Babies aren't something she's ever shown an interest in, Mum,' she says. 'She'll have to at least do some of it herself. How's she gonna cope, Mum? I won't be able to do *everything* will I?'

Nanny refuses to let me foster any babies. Not in her house. She doesn't approve of short-term fostering. Why bring a dear little baby in your home, invest time and love in it, only to have to give it up to its own mother as soon as you've grown attached?

In July, on the afternoon when the contractions come, I lock myself in the loo and refuse to come out. Nanny tries to reason with me and coax me out. I scream 'I'm scared, Nanny! I don't know how to have a baby!'

I hear Nanny shuffling away to pick up the phone and ring Wendy. Then she's back outside the bathroom door.

'Darling, Wendy's said Mick will have to come round and take the bathroom door down if you don't come out. We've got to get you to St Richard's. Be a big girl, Nin. Open the door.'

I open the door a crack and peer out at Nanny who is smiling gently at me. Sweating, I stagger out towards her.

'Come here, darling,' she says, reaching out to me.

I try to fall into her frail arms but my enormous belly bounces against her like a beach ball.

Two and a half hours later, I am a mother.

I open my eyes. Wendy is holding her – my daughter. She has a soft crop of curly black hair, skin the colour of roasted coffee beans and she is looking up at Wendy as though expecting something from her.

'Isn't she beautiful!' says Wendy.

She hands me the baby gingerly, as if afraid I might drop her.

The first thing I say is, 'Does my mother know she's here?'

Wendy says yes, that she's already slipped out and phoned my mother. That my mother had had nothing to say but 'This is a disgrace.'

My stepfather, Uncle Abejide sent his love, apparently. He wishes me luck.

I name the baby Alice, after Alice Walker.

I hold my minutes-old daughter and feel a magical, infinite store of love glimmer down on me. Like sunbeams warming my skin. Nothing else matters but this moment, this sensation. This feeling lasts for all of two hours. Reality then sets in. Like: Who the fuck am I? Anita Williams, Professional Dropout.

I've got ten pounds in my bank account. My academic qualifications are few and far between. I've shown no ability, so far, to hold down a nine-to-five job. I can barely think straight, even. No home of my own, of course. My most valuable possessions are my Nike trainers. Actually, *no*: my most valuable, precious possession as of now is this blameless freshly born beautiful baby girl. I feel sorry for her, my brand-new baby girl. I'm ready to collapse on my knees and apologise to her. I can't even keep house plants alive.

I leave St Richard's – Nanny picks me up. We go out for tea on the way home and we pretend that this was the future everybody had mapped out for me. That this is my destiny.

I go home to Nanny's bungalow and we set Alice's hand-me-down cot up in the corner of my bedroom.

Hassan somehow obtains my address at Nanny's. He sends a letter, asking me to ring him up straight away. The day after receiving his note, I leave Alice asleep in Nanny's arms and I go to the phone box and ring Hassan.

'I heard you had a baby,' he says.

'Who did you hear that from?'

'Did you have a baby or not?'

'I want to know who said I did.'

'Either you had a baby, or you didn't.'

Silence.

'I need to know if I'm a father or not,' says Hassan.

The pips go and I don't bother to put another in ten pence. I let the call disconnect.

I don't get it. So, yeah, Hassan got me pregnant, but so what? What does that have to do with anything? It doesn't occur to me that a father might want to see his child.

I'm sure it went down this exact way between my own mother and my father. From what I can fathom, my father heard 'on the grapevine' that I'd been born. After his maybe four-month marriage to my mother had already dissolved. My mother wasn't saying anything and, anyway, she was seeing somebody else by then. My father returned to his native Sierra Leone, never knowing me.

Ten years later Hassan, who I will have been trying to trace for years, writes to me again, at Nanny's bungalow. By chance I will be visiting Nanny and she will hand me the letter. 'I need to know whether you had a baby or not,' he will write. 'You never reply to my letters, but I pray you are reading this.' By the time I read those words, I will have developed a greater capacity to behave in a functional way – and Hassan will finally meet and get to know his daughter.

I am not a proper mother. I feel love, confusion and terror in equal measure. I go through the motions and my movements are robotic. I cradle baby Alice, I speak to her softly. But that's not enough, is it? I've even grown proficient at changing nappies – but so what? I feel numb, as if I'm fumbling and swishing around underwater. It's like motherhood is a language that cannot be translated.

'What am I supposed to do?' I ask Wendy, one afternoon.

'What do you mean, *do?*' says Wendy.

'Aren't I supposed to get a job or go out with my friends or do something?'

'You *are* doing something,' says Wendy. 'You're a mum now. You've got a beautiful little girl to look after and to love you.'

Wendy smiles at me. Or is she smiling at Alice?

August comes and my mother rings to say she's coming down to Fernmere to 'take a look at' my baby. Back in 1982, she vowed never to set foot in Fernmere again unless it was to dance on Nanny's grave.

But Nanny's still alive and so my mother will not come to the bungalow her granddaughter and I share with Nanny. We meet on relatively neutral ground – in Wendy's sitting room. My mother arrives with three of my uncles, and with Uncle Abejide. My new daughter is gorgeous, Uncle Abejide says.

My mother says, 'Why is the child so dark? How has my beautiful Precious given birth to this Idi Amin lookalike? Is the child's father one of those black-as-tar Ghanaian men?'

It is like being kicked backwards in time. I look at Wendy, willing Wendy to say something, to stick up for me, to slap my mother around the face or order her to leave. Instead – silence.

I hold Alice tight, hoping she has no awareness yet of her grand-mother's knife-like words.

'Well?' demands my mother. 'Who *is* the father? What is going on here? Doesn't this stupid girl know who made her pregnant? It must be some "Kofi" from Ghana. The child is so dark!'

I ignore her and so does everyone else in the room.

'I think Alice's hungry,' I say to Wendy.

'Well, feed her then love,' says Wendy, grinning as goofily as any newly minted grandmother.

'Feed her!' my mother repeats.

'Can I feed her up in your room, Wendy?' I say

'Course you can, love.'

Wendy understands my shyness about my body, my reluctance to breastfeed in public. And Wendy's daughter, Kelly also under-stands – when we're out and Alice gets hungry, Kelly shields me with her body and keeps an eye out to make sure no pervy old men are trying to sneak a look at my tits.

'What is this rubbish?' my mother says. 'Feed her here. Feed her!'

Wendy's adopted son Andrew watches my mother with awe and fear in his eyes, like he's watching the hard nut on the play-ground, happy he's not the target.

My mother chases me up the stairs and into Wendy's bedroom. Leaning dangerously against Wendy's wardrobe she says, 'Well you've flushed your future down the toilet now, haven't you? This is ridiculous and it makes me so angry! How can you become a mother when you're not even a grown woman?'

'I am grown! I'm nineteen now.'

'Exactly,' my mother says.

Before she leaves, my mother hands me a fat wad of notes 'for the baby'. I end up frittering away the cash on faddish, foolish baby clothes – a tiny lilac puffa jacket and a pair of baby Nike Air Jordans.

*   *   *

September passes by, humid. I sit in my bedroom cradling Alice, staring into space, sweating, swollen and immobile. On my bedroom floor is a bin liner filled with the day's dirty nappies. I'll walk it up to the public rubbish bin outside the shop in a minute. I can't dispose of too many nappies (or any other rubbish) in our bin because Nanny feels unable to let me handle the bin much any more, in case I forget to wash my hands afterwards and then spread germs around the bungalow.

Wendy says the situation's not satisfactory; that no doubt I'd qualify for my own council flat, now I'm a single mum. But in order to get one Nanny would have to write to the council saying she didn't want me living in her bungalow. Then I'd technically be homeless, forcing the authorities to provide housing. Nanny says, 'Not over my dead body.'

Nanny *does* want me here. The outspoken, rebellious, theiving teen I had become has receded, disappeared even, as far as Nanny's concerned. I've borne redemptive fruit. I've brought home a brand-new Nin. Alice, Nanny says, is the 'living spit' of me.

Alice is asleep in my arms. Nanny and I are watching *The Bill*.

'Isn't our little angel beautiful?' Nanny says.

She is. Alice has masses of soft black hair now and she can't seem to stop smiling. And yet, and yet . . . I feel almost afraid of her. It's as if she is somehow silently accusing me of something. I look at Alice and I remember myself when *I* was a child, when I was a scared little girl. I'm reminded of how unkindly I treated myself, how I hated myself and blamed myself for the bad things that happened to me then. And now, being Alice's mother seems to be forcing me to confront *me* and my own past and I don't feel ready to do that yet. Maybe not ever. It's like the rabid ghost of my childhood is chasing me, and the more time I spend masquerading as a mother, the more I feel compelled to try to run away.

*   *   *

One morning Wendy comes into my bedroom and finds me sitting at my desk, staring at my sleeping baby, crying so hard that my entire face is drenched.

'You need a break, love. I think you've got post-natal depression,' says Wendy. 'I'll take Alice for the day and you get some rest.'

I take Wendy's advice, and set off for Chichester for the afternoon, alone. When I return several hours later, my eyes are shining with adventure.

'I've decided to go back to college!' I announce. 'I start next Monday!

Indeed I've convinced the principal who kicked me out of college three years ago to reinstate me. I've promised him I'll be the most impressive A level student the college has ever seen and he's let me enrol for A levels in English, Film Studies and Law. Alice can come to Chichester with me each day; I'll entrust her to the college crèche from Monday to Friday. I've got it all planned out.

I half expect Wendy and Nanny to dissuade me but then I realise that, perhaps, they are so sick of seeing my morose face that they'll be relieved to see the back of me.

Wendy says she thinks it's a great idea. Nanny says she's proud of me.

'Alice's such a tiny baby,' Wendy says. 'I wouldn't feel comfortable with her being carted in to some crèche where the people there don't know her. How are you gonna manage with her and her buggy on the bus, love?'

'I'll manage,' I say, sounding more confident than I feel.

'Listen, love,' says Wendy. 'I'll child-mind her during the day for you, while you're at college.'

'Really?' I say. I run up to Wendy and hug her. 'Thank you!'

With each week that passes, I'm shrinking. Literally. For no reason I can fathom, I am losing enormous amounts of weight.

My pregnancy weight and the heft borne of years of comfort eating melts away. I drop from eleven stone to eight and a half stone and all at once I have cheekbones. My arms and legs are like pipe-cleaners. I feel more attractive than . . . ever, in my life. With each pound I lose I look more and more like my mother. With each pound I lose, I feel less and less motherly.

I watch Wendy cradling Alice. She makes mothering look as effortless as reading, as effortless as writing or walking or breathing. Wendy has grown plump over the years and she wears these hairy cardigans she buys from Marks and Spencer and when she holds you, it feels like you're being swaddled in cotton wool. Me, though, I am all skinny arms and long spindly legs and nervous energy. Despite my abundant breasts, poor Alice won't even 'latch on' properly and she has had to go on formula. She seems almost desperate to be weaned, and to go to Wendy, and who can blame her?

Having babies is something African women can do, but – from what I've seen in my life so far – it's only white women who can be truly maternal. My mother and all of the other African women who've sent their children to Fernmere over the years seem to feel natural indifference towards their own offspring, a casual disregard that makes it feel okay to advertise them and give them away to total strangers, to use violence when children become annoying. Can someone like me – a pseudo-African – really compete with Wendy when it comes to raising a baby properly and being a decent mother?

Slowly I begin to fall in love with my newfound slimness. In fact I reach a point where I can barely stop checking myself out in the mirror, fearing my attractiveness may dissolve and vanish as suddenly as it appeared. Nanny watches my physical transformation and observes without comment as I begin to to slowly fall in love with my body, with my sexual attractiveness.

Without explanation, Nanny begins to offer me more and

more food, getting up early to cook me fry-ups before I set off each morning to drop Alice off at Wendy's and catch the bus to college. When I decline the extra food Nanny warns me, 'Be careful, Nin. Men will know about you.'

'Know *what* about me?'

'That you've got a little baby, dear. They'll think if you've done it once, you'll do it again. They'll think you're a woman of easy virtue.'

Male students at college do pay me a lot of attention now – perhaps unsurprisingly given the outfits I've taken to wearing. In the mornings, when I catch the doubledecker to Chichester Tech, I'm glared at by the other girls, the Woodview girls, who are three years younger than me and studying for BTECs in hairdressing and beauty therapy. They're sensibly dressed in jeans and T-shirts. I rock up to the bus-stop in pum-pum shorts, platform heels and cropped sleeveless tops so short they barely cover my breasts.

While I dress in a way that rubs most other girls up the wrong way, I manage to make a new friend. Annabel. Annabel is easy about her sexuality and doesn't seem to have any hang ups.

I begin to wonder what it would be like to to act more like Annabel. How would it feel to toy with men instead of being their prey? I remember the days when boys felt, at best, sorry for me. When I was invisible. What would it be like to be in control and to be desired, not in a furtive, degrading way but rather in a majestic way. To feel beautiful and powerful.

There is only one way to find out.

Wendy's observed that I seem knackered and suggests that she takes Alice for the night, as it looks like everything's getting on top of me. I say I'll spend the evening revising. Instead, I wait until Nanny's asleep and then I climb out of my bedroom window, wearing a Benetton slip dress that barely covers my knickers. Nanny would hear the front door if opened it, but she won't my hear my bedroom window from where she's snoozing in her armchair.

I jog to the foot of Woodview where I meet Annabel, who drives us to London, to a nightclub, where we chat briefly to a hyperactive hip-hop DJ called Dave. Kool G Rapp and DJ Polo are doing a show.

On the dance floor, Annabel and I are approached by a man who asks us if we want to 'party' with Kool G Rapp and DJ Polo. Annabel says she's encountered this sort of thing before, that hip-hop stars have scouts at their gigs, searching for girls to introduce to the rappers. I'm not sure whether this means the scout thinks Annabel and I are pretty, or that we just look very easy.

Annabel and I sit in the limo with Kool G Rapp and one of his back-up dancers, Kenny, gulping Moet et Chandon. Kenny tells me I'm 'fine as hell' and I am so stunned that I cannot reply.

We arrive at the Hilton, where Annabel slinks off with Kool G Rapp and I'm left in the bar, talking to Kenny, the dancer. He says he grew up in the South Bronx. Kenny says he was there when everything kicked off and he tells me about it all. He knows Slick Rick and he knows Doug-E-Fresh. He became a break-dancer when he was ten. We talk until 2 a.m. and then we go to his room and have sex until five. When I reluctantly prepare to leave, telling him I've got to get back home, he says, 'Call me.'

Annabel drives us back to Sussex and I climb back in through my bedroom window. Later that morning, I sit in my law class, marvelling at this development. I can't believe I just had sex with someone and that I liked it and that I want to do it again. When my lesson ends I skip to a phone box and call Kenny in his hotel room.

'Who this?' he says.

'It's me!'

'Who's me?'

'Anita. From last night. I just wondered, umm, if you slept well.'

'Oh, you the sexy brown-skinned girl wit da long legs?'

'I guess so,'

'What's *up*? Listen, I'll call you back in a bit. Gimme your number right quick.'

'What time are you gonna call? It's just that I go to college. I'm not always home.'

It takes me the entire bus journey to Fernmere to realise I've just been given the brush-off. When it dawns on me, I don't mind. Even if it was for only one night, I finally understood what all the fuss about men and sex was about.

I get home to Woodview and Nanny says, 'Some young man with an American accent rang for you earlier, Nin.'

'OH MY GOD!' I scream.

I race to the phone box, with Alice in her pushchair and I dial the Hilton, only to be told that Kenny's checked out.

I write endless letters. I'm always at the post office in Chichester or Fernmere, pushchair in tow. Or at WHSmith's, gazing long-ingly at the expensive vellum stationery. The letters I write – to magazines, to pen pals – are my lifeline, my connection to the possibilities of the future.

In April, I get my first-ever byline in a newspaper, the *Fernmere Observer*. They assign me a story about a field on Woodview that's turning into a quagmire. The Woodview residents (not that I've noticed) are furious that the council's doing nothing about the state of their field. I head to Woodview with the photographer. The photographer makes a joke about us possibly being unsafe venturing into a cesspool like Woodview. I laugh at his joke and don't admit that I live there.

I write to *Vogue*, plucking a name from the magazine's masthead – Georgina Boosey, the managing editor. She sounds important, I think. Important and very posh. I doubt I'll hear back, but six weeks later, a letter arrives. I race around to Wendy's, Alice on my hip.

'Look!' I shout, thrusting the letter towards Wendy. 'It's

from *Vogue*! They want me to go in there for a month's work experience!'

I don't understand why Wendy doesn't look impressed. If anything, she looks bored.

'Do you understand what *Vogue* is? This is, like, beyond *anyone's* dream!'

'But haven't you already done enough work experience now at the *Observer*?' Wendy says. 'It's like this writing stuff's taking over, love.'

'How do you mean?'

'Well, you have to give up your own dreams, don't you? Now that you're a mother. You can't let this writing stuff take over. You can't do all this runnin' round writing if you're going to be a mum. You can't do both.'

And there it is. My answer.

One-Way Ticket

FOR FILM STUDIES A Level, we are doing coursework on modern African-American cinema. First, we watch and analyse *New Jack City*, *Straight Out of Brooklyn* and *Boyz N The Hood*. Then the film tutor delivers a lecture about a new black American director called Spike Lee and unveils *Do The Right Thing* on the huge projector screen in the lecture room. During the scene in the movie where Mookie turns his back on his racist white employers and helps trash their pizzeria, I feel as if each and every member of the all-white film studies class is watching me, and mistrusting me.

For the majority of students in the film class, black cinema is just a course module, but I am spellbound. Each time the film tutor asks the class a question – 'Why does the Ice Cube character pour alcohol onto the ground after his brother is shot?' or 'What were the factors motivating the elderly man to shoot Wesley Snipes' character at the end of the film?' – mine is the first hand to shoot up.

I screen and re-screen the films obsessively at home, on the rental TV and video-player in my bedroom. Never before have I seen black people of my own generation depicted in the movies and I feel almost as if I've made a discovery nobody else in Fernmere knows about. In fact, I probably have.

Alice is spending more and more nights as well as days at Wendy's. It's an unspoken agreement. A silent agreement that I'm so maternally incompetent that this move is for the best.

Obviously I don't really go out in the evenings, because, if I've got time and energy to spare it should be spent on Alice, not on gallivanting around with my mates. So I stay home with Nanny. Usually I'm in my bedroom, glued to the TV screen, watching films. By the end of my first year of A Levels, I've watched *Boyz N The Hood* more than fifty times and I'm still not done. One evening I ask Nanny if she'd like to watch *Boyz N The Hood* with me and she sits through it, almost jumping out of her armchair every time there's a gunshot.

'Isn't it brilliant? What do you think of it, Nanny?' I ask.

Nanny says that Angela Bassett's character's 'ever so pretty for a coloured girl' but that she didn't understand why the boys in the film kept shooting at each other.

I launch myself into student-hood with an almost deranged zeal, handing my essays in days before they are due. I stay up all night to study, just for the sheer joy of studying, and in the afternoons after college I stagger to my part-time job, half-asleep. Then I rev myself up with coffee and Korean ginseng capsules so that I can do yet more studying, deep into the night.

Nanny tells me I am doing a good job at juggling being a mum and being a student, but I know she is lying about the mothering part. I am the most distracted, inadequate mother that ever lived.

At the end of my first year of college and my first year of motherhood, I win the college prize for academic achievement. Alice stays home with Nanny while Wendy and my former social worker, Barbara, accompany me to the awards ceremony.

My English and Film tutors don't ask me whether or not I intend to go to university; they ask me *which* universities I'm applying to. I'm predicted three A grades at A Level. I play along and fill out an UCCA form just for the hell of it. Just because everyone else on my course is filling out UCCA forms. I try to keep things at least slightly realistic by only applying to universities relatively close to home – UCL, Sussex, Royal Holloway and Southampton. Then I throw caution to the wind and apply to Oxford.

The news of my Oxford application does not impress anyone. In fact, everyone I tell has the same query: what on earth do I think I'm playing at?

Nanny says, 'Oxford? The *university*?'

Nanny's son Dave and his wife Julia say that this is the most preposterous idea us lot in Woodview have come up with yet.

My English tutor, who's recently marked my coursework on Gloria Naylor and Toni Morrison, warns me that Oxford is not a progressive institution, that it's mired in the dark ages.

'Aren't A levels enough then?' says Wendy, one afternoon, when I arrive at her house after college to pick up Alice.

'Enough for what?' I ask.

'To get a good job and that.'

'I don't know really,'

No one in our Woodview family has gone anywhere near university and I doubt university will really happen for me either. But I don't let go of that delicate little thread of possibility.

I unfurl the scrap of paper that has my mother's latest phone number scrawled across it and I head to the phone box to ring her. It's been months since we've spoken – my mother never deigns to phone me.

'Oh, it's you,' she says.

I ask her what she thinks about the idea of me going to university and specifically to Oxford and she livens up slightly.

'You're hardly the first person in this family to be going to Oxford,' my mother says. 'It will be a piece of cake for you. You've always been brilliant.'

But she used to call me dull. 'Why would it be like a piece of cake for me?' I ask, wanting to prolong this unexpected affirmation.

'Don't you understand what people you come from?' my mother says.

'Not really,' I say.

My mother proceeds to remind me. She recites again, the family history and the phone box swallows up my coins and I feed more and more coins in. I listen and listen, but this time it's not just a fantastical story, it's a connection to my past, it's a window into where I came from.

Three quarters of an hour later, my head's filled with anecdotes about my great-grandfather, the *eze* or King from Igboland. He transcended the limitations his peers tried to impose on him. My great-grandfather came from a very ordinary family, made a fortune, lost a fortune, made his fortune again and became a local king at the end of the nineteenth century.

A few weeks later, at *Vogue*, I find a phone message waiting for me on my temporary desk there. 'Your foster-sister Wendy called to say "remember to buy more nappies for your daughter".'

I shudder, suddenly feeling horribly exposed. My mother has warned me never to reveal to any employer that I'm a single mum. 'Just because you're black, people are already making up their minds about you without even knowing what you're capable of,' she'd said. 'If you tell them you are an unmarried mother as well, don't expect any doors to ever be open to you.'

I put on a brave face and strut along the corridor like it's a catwalk, wearing my pum-pum shorts and faking confidence, calling out a peppy good morning to everybody. And later that day I tell the managing editor I need an afternoon off next week because I've got persistent toothache and need to get to the dentist. It's a lie. I'm really attending Alice's second birthday, held at the Grange leisure centre in Fernmere, organised by Wendy.

'Look at those gorgeous legs!' says a staff writer called Mimi. I beam at her and flush with pride. For somebody at *Vogue* to compliment your legs can only mean one thing. That your legs are what Nanny calls 'horribly thin'. This delights me. I actually feel like one of the models who grace the hallowed pages of *Vogue*. I'm down to eight stone, and I pride myself on eating only one meal a day and that meal invariably consists of a packet of crisps and a black coffee.

My task today is re-typing an editor's address book. It's a thick, luscious Mulberry filofax filled with names and home phone numbers of famous people whose work I've admired, like Martin Amis and Hanif Kureishi. I toy with the idea of scribbling Kureishi's number in my own filofax and ringing him up. But then I realise I've no idea what I'd say. Would I giggle nervously, say 'I loved the *Buddha of Suburbia*' and then hang up?

My work at *Vogue* is lowly, but I love it. Typing up other people's articles is the only written work I get to do. I'm a dogsbody, picking up fashion samples from fashion houses, making coffees, running errands for a very emotional fashion editor named Isabella Blow.

An oily young man named Rory, who looks like a sort of bloated Matt Dillon, hovers over my desk. His soft body spills over the waistband of his enormous Levi 501s. He asks me a whole lot of questions. It's like he doesn't believe – in fact, *can't* believe – that I am here. Rory won a writing competition and a week's work experience at *Vogue* is his prize.

He asks me where I went to school. I tell him and then ask him where his school was. Rory went to Harrow.

'Really? My cousin went to Harrow too,' I say, remembering Chinua Eze, the rather camp and startlingly posh cousin my mother used to sometimes bring to Fernmere to visit me.

Rory looks at me with renewed interest. And confusion.

I try to picture myself through Rory's eyes. A girl who looks like a Lewisham rude-girl and speaks like a Sloane. A black girl presumptuous enough to pitch up at *Vogue*, and sit here quite happily, amidst a sea of spoiled white faces, drawing further attention to herself by dressing like she's on her way to a rave.

'Where are you from?' Rory asks.

I know what he means – where are your *parents* from?

'I'm from Fernmere in West Sussex,' I reply.

Rory hovers, his eyes seeming to penetrate me.

It's a look I've encountered before. A look I will encounter again and again and again over the years. The look that comes when people's manners evaporate and their nosiness takes over and they start grilling me in a frankly rude way. As if they have the right to probe. As if they expect me to justify my presence, whereas theirs should be taken for granted.

'How long will you be at *Vogue*?' Rory asks.

'A month.'

His eyes seem to be asking, why are you here? Who are you?

I sit there smiling, thinking, 'I'm Anayo's great-granddaughter. That's who I am.'

I'm hiding in the loos, reading the Cliff Notes for *Paradise Lost*. I peer at my reflection in the mirror. I'm wearing far too much lipstick. And my hair – relaxed, tonged and greased – looked fabulous in the smeary mirror in my bedroom but in *this* mirror, inside the toilet on a British Rail train headed to Oxford, it suddenly appears wispy, see-through, embarrassing.

'Who are you trying to kid?' I ask my reflection. 'Why not quit now before you really humiliate yourself?'

It's not even as if I've prepared anything constructive to say to the professors at the interview. They're bound to grill me about *Paradise Lost*, as that's what I'm studying right now. And what can I say? That I'm not *feeling* Milton at all. Can I just rant at them about precisely why and how much I hate *Paradise Lost*?

I shove my Cliff Notes into my jacket pocket. I'm wearing a Next blazer, over a black lycra catsuit, with black patent Chelsea boots. Who on earth wears a catsuit to an interview at Oxford University? What was I *thinking?*

Someone hammers on the toilet door. I ignore it. I can't come out and reveal my presence on this train because I don't have a ticket and I don't have a reasonable excuse for not having a ticket. It's not as if I always travel like this. I did actually pay my train fares to my interviews at UCL and Sussex and Royal Holloway and Southampton. But now, I'm all out of cash. I've exceeded the fifty-pound overdraft limit on my bank account and I'm a hundred pounds in arrears to Wendy for childminding fees.

Another knock. A male voice. 'I know what you're up to in there.'

'Oh really? What am I up to in here, then? Besides going to the toilet?'

'Open the door,' the man says. 'Or I will open it myself.'

I reluctantly open the door.

'Yes?' I say, with mock indignation.

'Let's see your ticket then,' the outraged ticket inspector says.

I mumble a lie about losing my ticket.

'If you do not have the correct ticket,' says the inspector. 'I will have you arrested at Oxford station, by the British Transport Police.'

The railway has its own police force? Fuck. I think of the time earlier in the year when I was commuting to *Vogue*, when I wrote a cheque in payment for a train ticket, knowing the cheque was very likely to bounce, which it did. The transport police might even have a dossier on me. I'm finished.

The train pulls into Oxford. I open the train door tentatively and peer out. I see the inspector pointing at me, talking to a uniformed officer on the platform. I shrug resignedly and walk towards them. I walk slowly, as if I've got absolutely nothing to hide. And then I suddenly accelerate. I sprint past them both, past the ticket kiosk and through the exit, sail round the corner, and into Oxford.

*   *   *

I return to Woodview, from my round of interviews, elated and in love with what I've seen and heard at the universities, the scent of old books, the hushed voices. Institutions where reading and learning are not only taken seriously but are treated as a vocation. I am eager to tell Nanny about this new world I have just seen. I want to share with her how intimidated I felt when I arrived but how a surge of confidence appeared from nowhere once I was actually called into each interview.

I am greeted with near-silence from Nanny. She does not ask me all that much about how the interviews went. It's like I died and came back to life and Nanny's trying not to hear too much about what the other side looked like.

A few days after my return from my university interviews, I come home from college to find Nanny, who's now seventy-eight, weeping as she sits in front of the TV with Alice in her lap. Her entire countenance seems to have slackened since I've started talking about university. Her fondant pink flesh hangs wearily from her bones. The only things about Nanny that still seem fully alive are her gleaming silver hair, still styled in 1940s waves, and her pale, bright eyes.

'I knew it! I knew it!' she says. 'I knew all those universities would try their damndest to sign you up. I knew you could do it, Nin. But promise me, promise me you won't leave me, Nin.'

'Keep your hair on, Nanny,' I say, plucking Alice from her arms. 'None of the universities have actually accepted me yet.'

A few weeks later, my first offer letter arrives, from Sussex University. Followed by an acceptance from UCL. Then Royal Holloway. Then Southampton. Then University College, Oxford.

I ring my mother. It's the third time I've called her in two days. I'm becoming rather like a toddler clutching at a mother's sleeve, saying 'Look at *me*, Mummy! Look what I can do!' I dash to the phone box and ring up my mother every time I achieve anything. If this carries on I'll soon be ringing her up just to announce I've passed a bowel movement.

'Oxford has accepted me,' I say.

I imagine this is all I'll need to say for my mother to accept me too. She will finally consider me worthy of being her daughter.

'Accepted at Oxford for what?'

'To read English.'

'*What?*'

'English. It's always been my favourite subject. It's what I'm best at.'

'You'd better ring them up and ask them if they'll let you switch to medicine or law,' she says. 'What is the point of studying English? You already speak flawless English. What is a degree in English going to do for you? You have to be smart and make smart choices and work the system. Anyway, I've got to go. My sons have just come home from school. Later.'

My results arrive. I have an A in English. An A in Film Studies. And a C in Law. I run to the phone box to call my mother.

'You got a C in something,' she says. 'How did that happen? What subject?'

'The C's in Law. It just means I'm definitely not cut out to be a lawyer, I guess. I got As in the other two.'

I laugh. Feeling drunk on my success.

'I doubt Oxford will take you with that,' my mother says. 'You'd better call University College London and Sussex University and beg them to give you a place. Call me back if you manage to get any university to take you.'

'But Oxford asked for ABB, this is the same thing. It's the same number of UCCA points.'

'Same number of what? Call me back if you manage to get any university to take you now.'

Silence.

'Hang on a minute! How many A Levels exactly did *you* get, while raising a baby? Oh, wait a minute, you didn't raise most of your babies, did you?' I say suddenly, surprising myself.

'You don't know anything about me or what I've been through,' says my mother.

'I would if you'd tell me.'

'Focus on your own life. Make something of yourself. Just make something of yourself.'

'How do I do that?' I ask. 'What about Alice?'

'Leave her with Wendy,' says my mother. 'Let Wendy deal with the bother of training her. Alice will come back to you when you're ready for her, just like you came back to me, once you came to your senses.'

I sit in the blue armchair, opposite Nanny, waiting to hear from my mother. She has promised to drive me to Oxford.

'Do you mind me using the phone, Nanny? I'll only be on there for, like, two minutes.'

Nanny, who's feeding Jaffa Cakes to Alice, nods.

I ring my mother.

'What time are you getting here Mum?' I ask.

'Oh. I meant to ring you about that.'

'Are you running late?'

'There's something with my leg.'

'What's wrong with it?'

'It's paining me, Neety. I can't drive you today. But maybe by tomorrow it will feel better and I should be able to come then. I'm behind with everything. My sons are starving hungry. I haven't cooked yet. Talk later.'

Mick's parents have helped him invest in a nearly new Ford Sierra. Me, Wendy, Alice, my suitcases, my books, my kettle, stereo, hip-hop LPs and twelve pairs of trainers are packed into the new car. It's a sunny day but Oxford feels cold. Ghostly grey buildings casting out the sunlight, looming over the street. Traffic seems to dawdle, the cars moving in slow motion, slower than the bikes that weave up and down the streets.

Through the car window there's the sound of imperious foot-steps on a quaint street. The baby girl in my arms is as warm as a little oven. I smell the hair grease I've rubbed into her soft puff of hair. Her skin smells of cocoa butter. I rub my face against her face and feel tears not just pricking at my eyelids but welling deep inside me.

When we left Woodview this morning, Nanny's eyes were blank and red. She sat looking longingly at Alice and at me.

'You can't go to Oxford in that horrible old pair of jeans,' she said finally.

Then she curled a five-pound note into my jeans pocket and said, 'Here. Buy yourself something decent to wear when you get there. You never know who you might meet.'

While she was talking to me and putting the money in my pocket, I looked at the ground and then out of the window. I couldn't bear to meet Nanny's eyes. I had forgotten that I loved her until it was time to go. Before I left, the last words Nanny said were to Wendy. 'Make sure you don't let Oxford take my Alice away from me as well. I couldn't bear it. You make sure you bring at least one of my girls back to me, Wend.'

At Oxford, you have to live in college for the first two years and no children are allowed to live there. I'm not old enough to qual-ify as a 'mature student' and get a flat off-campus.

Wendy has offered to look after Alice during term time, although I've no idea how I'll contribute significantly towards Alice's keep as Oxford bans undergraduates from having part-time jobs during term-time and encourages us not to work during the holidays either.

Even as Mick's Ford Sierra hovers along the High Street, inch-ing ominously towards University College, I am not sure that I can go through with being away from Alice for months at a time. I am not sure if there is even any point in getting out of the car.

I speak silently, maybe to God, maybe to myself.

Please don't make me have to make this decision.

There has to be another way to forge a future for us both. Alice looks so serene in my arms, so sure of me, sure of everyone in this car. We, collectively, are her life. She loves and trusts each one of us. I squeeze her so tight that she looks up into my face questioningly. Will I turn back and become a proper mother to her, or will I become somebody else?

I will become a journalist. I will spend six years working in New York. I will have articles published in the *Daily Telegraph*, the *Financial Times*, the *Evening Standard*, *Elle*. I will find that you can run before you even know how to walk. I will spend years kicking open doors people would swear were shut to me. I will fight, fight, fight. And I will end up crippled, in a way. Never learning how to slow down. How to love. How to *feel*. There is room for only one in my parachute. I am not able to snap out of survival mode, at least not before it's too late.

I always wanted to be a journalist, but that wasn't my only goal. I had set out to become a sweeter, saner, more nurturing person than my own mother. For a while I imagined I'd achieved this and then some, simply because I did not beat up, deride or instil fear in my daughter – or in anybody else. I guarded my insecurities, my confusion about motherhood, my guilt, my self-doubt, my self-*hate* and I did not share any of it with anyone. I held absolutely everybody at arm's length. But I didn't see that as a problem. At least I wasn't *hurting* anyone. Or so I told myself.

It didn't occur to me until I was years older that in withdrawing, in being genial enough but closed, I was in fact inflicting cruelty – I was neglecting those I love and those who love me. I did not see this until I tried to slip into Alice's shoes. Until I tried to imagine how it must hurt when the woman who brought you into the world, the person who should love you more than anyone, remains indifferent and untouchable. How must that feel? And then I realised that I already knew precisely how that feels and that I had repeated a pattern without meaning to, before I had even come to understand that there *was* a pattern to repeat.

And thus by the time I have grown enough to have at least a vague idea of what being black and being a woman and being a mother might mean, it is too, too late. By the time I am emotionally mature enough and healed enough to step up to the plate and become a mother, my daughter is nearly the age I was when I gave birth to her; and by then she has a new mother. Wendy.

Wendy and Mick will save up, get a Right To Buy from the council, sell their council house and move to a middle-class cul-de-sac across the road from Woodview. Alice will have her own large bedroom there.

'They are never ever going to give that child back to you,' my mother will tell me, sounding at once bitter and smug. 'You'll never get her back now. This is what they wanted all along.'

I never do take Alice back. At first, Wendy said, 'I'm just not sure you're ready yet to be a mum, love.' And she was not wrong. But years tick by and Wendy and I begin to make excuses for my continuing incapacity: it's not fair to take Alice away from Fernmere, away from all her friends at the primary school. Away from everything she's ever known.

So it becomes a sort of slow-drip adoption. Alice gradually becomes Wendy and Mick's daughter, without any of us sitting down and having a deep conversation about what's happening. When the four of us are out together, Alice will call Mick 'Dad' and when she says 'Mum!' both Wendy and I will respond at the same time. Eventually, deciding I'm pointless, I'll stop showing up for sports days and other outings, leaving Mick and Wendy to take charge and leaving Alice feeling rejected.

In the years to come, Alice and I will reach a point where we only see each other for stilted dinners and occasional weekends away. With her and me, it's like the umbilical cord was never snipped, but rather left to fester, siphoning poison into our relationship.

One day, Alice will say to me, 'You make me sick. If I was a mother, I'd never choose a career over my precious child. You write all these articles and never once have you mentioned me in any of them. You disowned me. I think you've been a crap mother.'

'I agree,' I will say. 'And I am so, so sorry that I wasn't a better mother. I just want you to know that it wasn't because there was anything wrong with *you* – it wasn't anything you did at all, so please don't think that. It had to do with some stuff about me, and my past, that you don't know about.'

'I don't care,' Alice will say. 'I don't *care* about what happened to you in your life or what your mother did or didn't do. That's got nothing to do with me.'

On my first night at Oxford, fellow students, some of whom will become lifelong friends, want to know a bit about me.

'Who were those people?' they ask. 'That white couple? Who was that gorgeous little baby?'

And I will say, at first, 'Oh that's my little girl. Alice. Those are my sort-of parents. They're looking after my daughter for me while I'm here.'

'Yeah, right,' one of them will say. 'Tell the truth – she's your kid sister! Are they your adoptive parents?'

'Yes, I'm adopted,' I lie. It sounds tidier, more respectable. I'm adopted – and Alice is my baby sister.

I place a framed photo of Alice, wearing a white dress, on the antique desk in my oak-panelled room.

'She's *sooo* cute,' says the man who will become my boyfriend.

And this is the image of Alice I will carry with me. A two-year-old with glowing ebony skin and huge liquid brown eyes that are still soft, still trusting. I shut this image of my baby away inside an imaginary box tucked inside my heart and I truly believe she will remain there, suspended in time until I am ready to mother her.

Mick pulls up outside the porter's lodge, opens the car door and looks around him.

'This is the real thing, innit?' he says. 'Oxford bleedin' University.'

The look on Mick's face reminds me of the expression I've seen him sport on the rare occasions he's required to go to church, for a wedding or a christening. Reluctance and reverence and a flicker of resentment. Mick looks about him warily. He sees old, tall grey buildings everywhere and the one where I'm going is one of the oldest and greyest in the town.

Alice is growing sleepy. I kiss her on the neck.

I have never reached out to somebody and asked them for help and wholeheartedly expected them to give it before. I've always assumed people wouldn't be there for me. But now I reach out to my daughter. *Please Alice*, I tell her silently. *Don't ever stop loving me.*

There's a kebab van parked just ahead of Mick's Sierra.

'At least you won't starve or nothing,' Mick says, nodding approvingly, laughing. 'Oh I forgot, you don't eat nothing do you? Bloody weirdo.'

'I *do* eat now.'

And I *am* eating, finally: I eat two proper meals a day, sometimes three. My weight's stabilised at nine stone.

'She don't want to end up looking as fat as us two, do you Neet?' says Wendy, shutting the car door with her hip. 'Don't wanna end up like us, do you?'

I can't answer her. There's so much to say. I *do* want to be like Wendy and Mick, in a way. In fact, I'd like to go back to Fernmere with them. I'd like to climb back into the Ford Sierra and sit there holding Alice as we cruise back to Fernmere.

But isn't it already too late to go back? Doesn't Wendy already think that I think I'm better than her? That I am expecting far too much from life; that I'm childishly, stubbornly, refusing to accept my lot? I am pretending to myself that I am leaving Woodview only for the duration of each eight-week term at Oxford. But this isn't true. Fernmere will never really be my home again. Nanny will go into a nursing home. The bungalow on Woodview she and Alice and I used to live in will be rented to another old lady.

Mick's apprehensive laugh seems to echo as we approach the Porters' Lodge.

A grim-faced porter looks at the four of us with open curiosity.

'Precious Williams,' I say.

Alice giggles at this because Little Precious is the nickname I occasionally use for her when we're out on one of our Saturday afternoon trips, eating tea cakes in tea shops in Chichester. 'Do you want Mummy to get you another tea cake, my little precious,' I sometimes say, hoping that she will say 'No, I'm full, Mummy,' because I have so little money.

'You all right, love?' says Wendy, rubbing my arm with hands roughened-up by years of hair-dressing.

'Calling yourself Precious now, are we?' says Mick, smirking.

Precious: that is my name. But my foster family will always call me Anita. Doesn't matter that my birth certificate and my passport say Precious. Wendy, Nanny, Mick – they won't seem to accept Precious. In months to come, my new Oxford friends will phone me during the holidays.

'Hi, can I speak to Precious, please?'

Nanny will say, 'I'll get Anita for you.'

'Hi Wendy, it's me, Precious.'

'Oh, hello, Anita.'

Precious will be the writer, the grown woman, the adventurer. Anita, in my eyes, was the baby given away, the teenager raped on a toilet floor. Anita is the elephant in the room and while

I pretend she doesn't exist, my foster-family will interact with Anita and *only* with Anita. They don't understand that I killed Anita off years ago. And I do not understand yet that the me I once was is still waiting for her mother to love her the way she wants to be loved, so that she can love her own daughter the way her daughter needs to be loved. So that she can be present.

The porter is now staring. We are a spectacle.

'I'm Precious Williams,' I say again.

The porter nods.

My name is on the list.

ACKNOWLEDGEMENTS

Thank you to Maya Angelou, Zora Neale Hurston and Alice Walker for opening my eyes; to Nanny for encouraging an early love of the written word; and to Alexandra Pringle, Anna Simpson and the wonderful team at Bloomsbury for encouragement, expertise, patience, support . . . for believing in me and in this book.

Thanks too to Arabella Stein. And with love to my niece. A special thank you to Wendy for opening up to me about my past, enabling me to shine some light into the dark recesses of my childhood.

Finally, writing this book was, at times, a terrifying experience. I'd like to thank everyone who supported me and gave me love and understanding during the writing process.

A NOTE ON THE AUTHOR

Precious Williams is a former contributing editor to *Cosmopolitan* and her personal essays and celebrity interviews have also appeared in the *Telegraph*, *The Times*, the *Guardian*, *Wallpaper*, *Elle*, *Marie Claire* and the *New York Post*. She lives in London.

A NOTE ON THE TYPE

The text of this book is set in Linotype Goudy Old Style. It was designed by Frederic Goudy (1865-1947), an American designer whose types were very popular during his lifetime, and particularly fashionable in the 1940s. He was also a craftsman who cut the metal patterns for his type designs, engraved matrices and cast type.

The design for Goudy Old Style is based on Goudy Roman, with which it shares a 'hand-wrought' appearance and asymmetrical serifs, but unlike Goudy Roman its capitals are modelled on Renaissance lettering.